PREMISE 1

After readi  ?
beginning writer, t
conducting researc
down, you find yo,
prospect of conducting your own research, then may you be
motivated completely—and I encourage you to do so—to
state openly to the world that humankind needs yet to find a
better means of understanding and describing, with anything
amounting to lasting accuracy, our fellow humans and the
planet we share. You see, research excites me because it is so
damnably perplexing and dangerous. When used responsibly,
research can elevate the whole of humanity, but when used
irresponsibly, research will devalue another person or social
group's humanity. Thus, research is humanity's friend and
enemy at the same time.

Research is thought by most people to provide us
with facts, which are considered essential to a basic
understanding of life and life's realities. On the other hand,
facts are by nature suspect. Yes, facts can be discovered
objectively, or neutrally (as in, "The water is 75-degrees.");
however, the same facts are more often than not shaped
subjectively to suit a **rhetorical**, or persuasive, purpose (as
in, "The water is lovely. You should come in."). And if facts
can be suspect, then so can the stated truth because, again,
truth is thought by most people to be based on the
accumulation of facts. This last point terrifies me, and it
should terrify you, too. Just think, only about 100 years ago
public education was thought to be wasted on women (of any
race) and African-Americans, in general. Anthropological
science had thought itself to have "proven" the brains of
females and people of color were different enough in
function and mass from the "ideal" Caucasian male brain that
the two were classified as one or two steps above mental
retardation; the nexus of the two groups, the African-
American woman, then, was "known" by science to be the

least-advanced human. Of course, and rightfully, this junk science has since been tossed into the garbage can of history. But what is suggested when the bulk of each generation's "truths" are written only to be deleted like so many now-unwanted text messages?

Research is far less about the evolution of ideas and much more about the arrangement of ideas to suit explicit and implicit purposes; the respected Scientific Method is flawed at heart because the observations and fact checking the Method depends upon are founded upon necessarily subjective human observations and analyses. Even those devices and machines designed for the purpose of assisting neutral observation and analysis (for example. the survey, computer, and the electron microscope), designed as they were by humans, skew reality often. A researcher has an obvious, vested interest in the success of her study and its data collection; the computer will perform only those tasks it was programed by a human to do; and the very electricity put off by an electron microscope will cause an electron under a researcher's observation to shift its orbit from its natural path. The researcher's fingerprint is, therefore, most everywhere. Returning to my previous example of the human brain, I sense the intellect of females and people of color is seen now as equal to that of the Caucasian male less because it is the right thing to do—the history of emancipatory philosophy aside, **material**, or actual, human life has only very recently included practical application of a sense of fairness—and more because of the groundswell of 21st Century liberal populism. Put simply, had American eugenicists and their implicit allies, the German National Socialists (the Nazis) been victorious, the earlier and racist data contained in our textbooks would not have changed, and the "truth" would have remained unaltered because it would have conformed to a world view held by a dominant social power. Subjective perception, then, has as much bearing on research as does what we would like to call our objective search for the truth does.

Consider analysis of the recent Michael Brown debacle. At heart, the incident centered on the fatal shooting of one man, a civilian, by another, a police officer on patrol. Shortly after the event, the American press altered its first description of the incident with the addition of provocative adjectives and the elimination of fundamental data, from the racially-neutral 'man suspected of a robbery shot fatally during a later confrontation with a police officer', to the racially-charged 'white officer killed unarmed black youth'. The nature of the catalyst, the alleged smash-and-grab robbery that saw a store clerk thrown to the ground, was altered as well; the press began describing the initiating action as the more minor infraction of shoplifting. Thus, initially, the press fostered three **competing narratives**: 1) robbery suspect killed; 2) unarmed black youth killed; and 3) black shoplifting suspect killed. The first and last narratives were dropped quickly; most any mention of catalyst seemed to disappear when the press made the choice to remove its initial selection and presentation of Brown's Facebook "selfies" showing him with angry facial expressions to those showing him to be a happy, smiling teenager. Having made the choice to remove the incident's **underlying context**, the press freed itself to focus on the incident's **pathos**, emotion, almost exclusively. The rhetorical obviousness of this choice is clear; the racially-charged headline 'White officer killed unarmed black youth' will sell far more newspapers and will increase radio and television ratings that greater numbers of listeners and viewers provide exponentially. The addition of numerous interviews with Brown's grieving mother and father calling for the white police officer's arrest, and the almost-complete deference given to the parents' subjective opinion, combined with a fourth inserted narrative, that Brown was merely enjoying a stroll in his segregated neighborhood before leaving for college, served to emphasize what can be considered the press' profit-driven race baiting. Activists for and against Brown took the press' lead and reshaped the incident to suit their own purposes.

Pro-Brown activists, for instance, shaped the incident's description into a fifth narrative, which read, 'white officer murdered black youth' and adopted the rallying cry of "Hands up, don't shoot!", thinking mistakenly, or wanting to believe, these were Brown's last words. Since the police officer's grand jury hearing, pro-Brown activists introduced sixth and seventh narratives: 'Brown's death is representative of law enforcement's fondness for the use of excessive force' and 'it is 'open season' on black men.' Interestingly, it was at with the pro-Brown activists' seventh narrative that anti-Brown activists attempted to take the rhetorical lead actively with what they thought were **logical**, or data-driven, appeals; earlier, they invested most of their time in calling on the public to wait for the grand jury's decision and the court's dissemination of sworn testimony. Calling to mind white suspects are shot more often by police than black suspects, at a rate of roughly 3-to-1, anti-Brown activists suggested the pro-Brown movement's **pathetic**, or emotion-driven, appeals are less truthful than what factual evidence can provide. Anti-Brown activists also put forth the ideas, Brown had stolen drug paraphernalia (cigar wrappers are used for the purpose or rolling marijuana often), Brown was high during the alleged robbery (the young man's postmortem drug test confirmed his state of chemical intoxication), and the altercation with the officer would have been avoided had Brown not punched the officer when questioned.

Thus, the public was left to digest an eighth narrative, which showed a drug-addled ruffian, who at least on that day lived by violence, and died as a result of his violence. Though Brown's mother initially denied it was her son on the store's videotape of the alleged robbery, after the grand jury ended she admitted it was. Even so, and as a means of counter-argument to anti-Brown activists, pro-Brown activists suggested in a ninth narrative any mention of Brown's drug abuse is inappropriate, that the term, 'thug' is racist, and the only **material**, or relevant, fact is a black youth had been executed summarily, without benefit of public trial. Brown's stepfather called for the neighborhood to be burned down, and the press seemed now to limit its commentary to describing associated protests as peaceful or not.

We then see Brown's death can mean anything we want it to mean. Today's press seems to be interested more in **subjective perceptions**, where opinion and fact are given equal weight, than in **objective analyses** in search of one truth; perception and reality are taken often to be one-in-the-same. If we take journalists to be researchers, we are compelled then to question the weight we give to research. Can, for instance, a human ever be depended on to research in a **wholly objective**, or non-biased, manner? Or, perhaps, are news media almost perfect examples of art imitating life inasmuch the American populace is an opinionated bunch who like having pundits more than reporters; pundits, who, rather than presenting strait forward news, present accepted editorialized 'truths' to readers, listeners, and viewers? Here we must remember news does not come to us in an unfiltered stream; rather, editors and corporate producers choose to present only those stories they consider to be most 'newsworthy', and by newsworthy they mean important, of 'known' public interest, and capable of increasing advertising revenue. Then again, perhaps news media workers are merely self-aware of the fact they exist in a postmodern world, and perhaps they are more self-aware of this than other researchers, like academics and scientists in the public and private sectors.

Premise 1 Review Questions:

What can the term, "material," refer to?

Explain the difference between "objective" and "subjective."

Why will many people believe what they see in the news?

PREMISE 2

Postmodernism refers to what is possibly the most encompassing philosophy today, yet its name suggests the viewpoint's comparative youth. Meaning "after modernism", postmodernism sprung largely unto the world stage as a critical social response in 1945, at the conclusion of World War II. It is a guiding system of **analytical**, or dissecting, questions, which strove initially to **deconstruct** and understand this catastrophe brought about by the Nazi Germans, Imperial Japanese, and other Axis powers; we tend to forget over 50 million people died during this six-year war. More specifically, postmodernism is so interesting because rather than affirming humanity, in spite of the War, the philosophy centered itself on a negative **stasis**, or standpoint. Remember, prior to the Second World War, and during the Modernist Period, humankind had almost a limitless faith in science and its social benefits. However, this same science produced the Nazi death camps, which murdered on an industrial scale in Europe, the biological weapons (and associated vivisections of civilians during their research) the Imperial Japanese Army used in its attempts to quell Chinese resistance, the bombers all sides used to terrorize each other's civilian populations, and the atom bomb the Americans employed to bring the Japanese Empire into final submission. Thus, postmodernism reckoned, if the height of modernist science showed itself not to be the deliberate elimination of disease, hunger, and poverty, but rather the calculated escalation of death, ignorance, and want, then perhaps science is concerned more with the harnessing of power for power's sake than in pursing unselfish knowledge whilst doing no harm. We must then, postmodernism asserts, be distrustful of science and consider scientists as generally the agents of corporate, governmental, or military interests. The world was also a far more religious place prior to 1939, when the Second World War started.

Given the sheer vastness of the War's destruction, the Theodicy Question—why God allows bad things to happen to good people—became paramount. The analogous questions of 'Where was God?' and 'Why was God silent?' during the Holocaust in Europe and the endemic cannibalization of civilians, enemy combatants, and fellow soldiers by the Japanese Army (who were provided with few supplies and ordered to live off of the land) in their Chinese, New Guinean, and Philippine possessions rendered the most common explanations offered by clergy, that 'God works in mysterious ways' and 'Humans are too dim to understand God's purpose', vague and unsatisfying at best. Postmodernism, therefore, called on humankind to question its ancient dependence on belief systems centering on the intangible, like religions. Here, and importantly, as a philosophy postmodernism did not put forth an alternative to God in the form of the human individual; after all, the Nazis did just that with their elitist superman concept. Nor did postmodernism suggest a return to animistic or most basic forms of religion as the Imperial Japanese manipulation of Shintoism had its populace believing it was descended uniquely from the Sun, and thus, of genetically better stock than other, 'less heavenly', peoples; the latter considered then worthy of Japanese domination. No, postmodernism was content to remind humankind that when tens of millions of innocents were murdered in the name of ethnic difference and global domination, God had seemed to have gone fishing.

Lastly, and beyond science and religion, postmodernism threw suspicion on placing too much faith on the popular idea of cultural advancement. Case-in-point, prior to the Second World War, the world saw Germany as a most rational nation; the country was considered almost an unquestioned leader of the arts, intellectualism, the sciences, and social order. Similarly, Japan was thought of by most as the home to beauty and the soul of personal discipline. So, after the world became especially shocked by Germany's fanatical, 'scientific' attempt to create a race of supermen at the cost of so-called 'racial enemies' and Japan's terroristic program of mass rape and disemboweling of colonial women (even Hitler had called on the Japanese Army be less severe during The Rape of Nanking, the destruction of China's then-capital), postmodernism suggested the world's collective disappointment was more than a little naïve; the Axis powers had, after all, stated their shared subjective disdain for empathy, let alone sympathy, publically and often. And one group's ability to empathize with another group is dependent on the former's equal desire to consider experiences belonging to the latter objectively. Postmodernism held it was not as if Hitler or his Japanese counterpart, Tojo had merely flipped switches when they came to power, that the two so-called most culturally advanced nations descended into evil and selfishness overnight. Rather, postmodernism implied, Hitler and Tojo tapped easily into urges most all peoples share implicitly, if not explicitly: **homogeneity** and **rigidity**. Put simply, the Nazi plan coalesced around a policed, unified community and the Japanese samurai code had as its basis a zealous unwillingness to disobey any order given by social superiors. It was easy to know one's place in either of these regimes because the need for critical thought was eliminated; the Nazi German and Imperial Japanese governments 'did the thinking' for their respective citizens and subjugated peoples. As a result, postmodernism attempted to deconstruct the very idea of individual identity wholly.

Because the Nazi Germans and Imperial Japanese centered identity on singular 'genetic' or group **binaries** (that is, you possessed 'Aryan' features or you did not, you were racially a superior being (*'übermensch'*) or an inferior being ('*untermensch*'), Japanese or '*marutai*' (a piece of wood), worthy of existence or slated for extinction), postmodernism **decentered** exclusionary notions of identity to include an almost limitless set of **descriptive variables**. According to postmodernism, identity is based on, but not limited to, one's personal identification with age, appearance, biological sex, economic class, education, ethnicity, gender, history, physical ability, politics, race, region of origin, religion, sexual identity, social class, and so on. Thus, while postmodernism did not shift description of the individual from the subjective to the objective, it did shift ownership of biased description from a power structure or social group to the individual; the 'You are…' of yesterday became the 'I am…' of today. In other words, though some may regard me, for example, as "too old", postmodernism allows me, more importantly, to declare publically "I am only as old as I feel". Postmodernism continues to look down upon essentialism and alterity today.

Premise 2 Review Questions:

What does the verb, "analyze," mean?

What does the verb, "decenter," mean?

Do we, in fact, live in a postmodern world?

PREMISE 3

Essentialism is the idea a **discrete**, or limited, set of variables (for instance, reproductive organs possessed, amount of melanin held in the skin, and class and cultural backgrounds) can define, and most crucially, unify peoples who are said to share the same variables. Here, postmodernism runs into significant, **existentialistic** conflict with the various feminisms and ethic awareness and power groups. Yes, at their core, each of the feminisms (there are over a dozen kinds) call for the end of racism and sexism, and the betterment of men and women alike through the active and policed **reformation** of historically oppressive social structures and learned interpersonal behaviors. However, postmodernism asserts, because the feminisms are founded essentially upon the idea that women share largely the same physiology, history, and economic ambition, and that women can unify for shared biological, cultural, monetary, and political ends, the feminisms continue to be more similar to outdated, pre-1945 modernist movements than anything truly revolutionary. Postmodernism tells us the feminisms today continue to answer the question, 'What is a woman?' without the necessary effort a post-Second World War planet demands. For example, whereas the earliest incarnations of American feminisms recognized imposed gender and sex differences as only necessary starting points (to understand how we may come together, we must first understand how we were driven apart), the movements today seem to embrace and celebrate social difference. On the other hand, postmodernism sees the idea of difference more of a matter of subjective perception than **material** or actual reality. That is to say, given the sheer diversity of life, postmodernism questions if gender, and even biological sex differences, beyond cultural assumptions exist truly.

Postmodernism considers **explicit** or visible biological sex differences as superficial and a matter of illusion. For example, to the eye, male and female external reproductive organs appear differently; however, postmodernism reminds us, through a microscope, we see the cells forming the clitoris and the penis' glans are the same. Likewise, both structures become erect during arousal's vasocongestion or blood rush. The most basic anatomical sex 'differences', therefore, are merely little more than the rearrangement of the same human tissue, and one may consider sexual intimacy shared between humans more as homoerotic than heteroerotic (the prefixes 'homo-' meaning same and 'hetero-' meaning different). Consequently, postmodernism places the designation 'human' as more accurate and important than 'male' or 'female', and seeks to **shift** meaning away from conversations surrounding traditional binaries and social response movements. When one considers the feminisms cannot exist without the presence of sexism (just as atheism cannot exist without religion, nor black power without white power, nor Satanism without Christianity, nor class consciousness without economic or social classes, etc.), postmodernism suggests intellectual energy is spent better on investigating social problems as human problems; one cannot be put down with the statement "You run like a girl" if the concept of 'girl' does not exist (and incidentally, "girl" is a Scots word which referred once to a child of any sex). To be said to "Run like a human" is, then, quite a decentering, revolutionary statement as, at base, it is subjective (Which human? There is an almost infinite variety of humans.), and it counters preconceived, imposed cultural ideas ('Girls possess less physical ability than boys'.). But therein lies the rub: postmodernism takes the feminisms to task for seeing women as more-or-less the same, and with the same interests; however, postmodernism states also it is almost impossible for people not to picture the world in the ways the way they want to.

For example, the feminisms are explicitly about bringing forth the freedom and opportunity for women to be, and do, what they want to in what has become a **patriarchal**, or male-centered, world. Likewise, the feminisms hold, males can only benefit from complete female liberation because sexism, like racism, retards the emotional, intellectual, and social maturities of the oppressor as much as the oppressed. However, postmodernism asks, because the feminisms are identity movements as well, in what ways are the women who do not conform to feminist identities **rarefied**, or policed, by feminists? Likewise, do the feminisms consider nonconforming females as somehow less than 'real' women? As naïve? As willing slaves to males and male 'needs'? Think of historical feminist slogans: "If you are not a feminist, you are a masochist" (one who takes pleasure from pain; think of the pulp novel, *50 shades of Grey*), and "A woman needs a man like a fish needs a bicycle"; I have seen a photograph of my mother wearing a t-shirt stating the latter whilst holding me as a toddler in the early 1970s. Put simply, postmodernism calls to mind not all women want to be career women, but some do, not all women want the pressure of balancing career and family, but some find the challenge exciting, a number of women want to have husbands and children, but some find the idea of getting married or being a stay-at-home mom horrible, that some women find submissiveness attractive while others are repulsed by the idea, and many women go to college simply because at the end of the day, they want to find work, like male students, and do not care if females are allowed access into university today largely because of prior feminist activism (forgetting the 'question' of whether females could be educated was at play in America a mere 115 years ago). Thus, postmodernism's greatest complaint with the feminisms is the unthoughtful, identity-based social pressure applied to some women who embrace non-feminist subjectivities, a pressure reminiscent of the **vulgar**, or deliberate, power moves expressed historically by the very racist and sexist groups the feminisms **contest**. Further, postmodernism suggests, life's subjectivities doom the feminisms to **fracture** even more. Today there are more than a dozen feminisms, from movements which call for self-segregation from men to those which call for integration with men, from anti-pornography movements to pro-pornography movements, and from members who were thought to have burned their bras as a rejection of male domination 40 years ago to popular entertainers today, like Beyoncé, who twerk in the name of feminism.

Postmodernism's disagreement with the feminisms is not total, however. It, like the feminisms, seeks to decenter what is known commonly as 'the male gaze'; then again, postmodernism seeks to challenge through social critique all social definitions put forth by all power structures, dominant or not. So, because **the male gaze** refers to a sense of gender-based entitlement, expressed by how men in power, scientists in particular, have defined the view of womanhood historically, and by how these men continue to shape overall society's perception of women, postmodernism finds a common target. For example, it was men who defined the binaries of what are 'ladylike', 'feminine', and 'passive' as opposed to 'manly', 'masculine', and 'dominant', and it was men who came up with pejorative names for people who did not fit easily into either of the two assigned categories (for example, 'sissy', 'tomboy', and 'queer'; queer meaning strange). Further, it was men who defined, and continue to describe, the male as the stronger sex biologically, although it is now known widely that female infants suffer far less infant mortality than male infants, that female children are larger and mature faster than male children, that women live longer than men, and the act of childbirth would likely kill a man—the adult male's generally greater muscle mass proving to be no advantage at all here. Further still, men described themselves and maintain the image of themselves as the initiators of romance, as more potent sexually, the role of penetrator being seen as most important, despite the biological reality women, and not men, are capable of almost limitless staying power and orgasm. Such is the male fascination with male sexual power, postmodernism asserts, that it informs the day-to-day vulgarity of many American men; one stumbling upon a conversation between a few juvenile males could be forgiven if one believed a homoerotic film was being televised. Even the 'tamest' vulgarities, 'you suck' and 'get bent', refer to one being a felator and one being made ready to be penetrated, respectively.

Nevertheless, postmodernism, as a system of analysis, is more innocent than the feminisms as each of the varieties have, like most other social movements, political ambitions. And politics make for odd partnerships. As much as the feminisms protest the male gaze in science, they will make active use of scientific data, which move forward causes now important to them, like Lesbian, Gay, Bisexual, and Transgender (LGBT) rights. It goes without saying males outnumber females in the scientific professions, particularly in the arena of sex research (one would be surprised at the number of male sex researchers with Hyman as a first name), however, the feminisms have yet to question popular research suggesting at least half of American women are bisexual, despite the many studies' commonly small (typically less than a dozen volunteers) and biased (typically 50-percent self-describe as lesbian or bisexual) samples. Moreover, the feminisms seem unbothered these data continue to be collected with a male-invented electronic Doppler probe known as the vaginal photoplethysmograph, used to measure vaginal [blood] pulse amplitude (VPA). In this context, this probe is considered by sex researchers and feminists alike to be a completely **objective**, or neutral, tool. Beyond objectivity, the male gaze in these studies is thought to be removed, in part, as male researchers assign the task of inserting the probe into volunteers to female research assistants exclusively. Yet, use of the same blood-flow probe was called intrusive when its employment was considered by state governments in pre-abortion physical examinations, putting forth male scientists have had access to the female body and female sexuality for far too long.

Postmodernism is, however, concerned less with a study's sample size—researchers have long known the more **intrusive**, or personal, a study is, the fewer volunteers will participate in it it—and is concerned more with how the study's data are interpreted, and for what political and social purposes these data are used. Why, for instance, would the feminisms be interested in studies which put forth the idea half of American women are bisexual? Postmodernism would say it is mostly about continued growth of membership. Since the Nineteenth Century, the feminisms have advocated for historically othered, or disempowered, social groups. By attempting now to 'prove', through science, more people belong to such out-groups than ever imagined, the feminisms seek to remain relevant in a world made already somewhat more equitable by earlier feminists. Considering the **pragmatic**, or practical, sense aligning with these data makes (after all, a large number of young women today believe themselves to be so freed from sexism they consider feminism redundant and the word, 'feminist,' an insult), postmodernism cites the feminisms as not so different than other institutions inasmuch it is the goal of any institution to keep itself alive.

Put simply, the antagonism postmodernism and the feminisms appear to partake in stems from: 1) Postmodernism's general refusal to see the state of being a woman as necessarily unique to the human experience (or to see womanhood as more than another social construction in need of reconsideration and deconstruction); 2) As the feminisms were gaining social momentum, postmodernism was thought to have acted as a wet blanket when it criticized the feminisms' embracing of identity politics; and 3) Postmodernism has as its purpose the complete re-contextualization of social reality, and not the limited use of **semantics**, or word handling, to separate domineering male subjectivity from female experience, no matter how revolutionary new wording may appear. For example, changing the words, "woman" to "womyn" or "wombman" or "history" to "herstory" or "his story" attempt to shift a sexist worldview linguistically, and thus cognitively, but given these rewordings make their way out of Women's Studies classrooms, Facebook posts, or Afro-centric memes only very seldom, postmodernism holds the changes have yet to capture the larger public's imagination. Again, postmodernism does not take issue with rewordings or self-naming as means of self-acceptance and the start of great cultural shifts. Rather, postmodernism considers such actions as worthy only if doing so is not merely more historical delineation or boundary making. Remember, the feminisms, in general, did not consider the lesbian experience to be equivalent to the heterosexual female experience in the 1960's and 1970's (but now do), and currently the question of whether female-identifying transgendered individuals can claim to know the female experience is being 'debated.' Thus, the pronoun "her" remains a proverbial football inasmuch as the feminisms have yet to "decide" to whom the word can be passed to.

Premise 3 Review Questions:

Are the terms, "practical" and "objective," interchangeable?

How are the terms, "male gaze" and "patriarchy," related?

What impact does essentialism have on daily life?

PREMISE 4

We are beginning to see the inherent difficulty that words – their origins, purposes, and assigned tasks – present to humanity. People depend upon words to express themselves explicitly
(Though about 80-percent of our language is nevertheless implicit body language), but our vocabularies tend to come up short; words fail us often. So rare is our ability to think of, or speak, or write, the perfect word at the perfect time that 19th Century French writers coined a name for this rare find, *le mote juste*. We search for the perfect word, or even the right word, from birth until death. Postmodernism considers our common inability to match thought with word to be the beginning of vast emotional and intellectual valleys that separate one individual from another, going so far as suggesting each human is like one distant universe from

another: We can see each other, and know the other is there, but we will never know the other completely, even a close acquaintance of several decades. In other words, if you cannot describe what you feel or know, or yourself, completely, how can you expect a person other than you to be better able to articulate your feelings, thoughts, or being? And this assumes words and phrases which can give voice to our thoughts exist in the first place.

A lack of words, for instance, was central to one of The Holocaust's greatest tragedies. Because the very scale of the institutionalization and mechanization of this mass murder was so new to humanity, at least in Europe, its victims and survivors were at almost a complete loss to describe what they faced. Short of words for what was being seen in the ghettoes and death camps, prisoners were left to use the language of their Nazi captors, who, history recalls, had a sadistic sense of humor. Thus, "sport" came to refer to a sentence of death by exercising physically in place; "Rose Garden" meant a place of execution; "Canada" stood for the place where belongings stolen from incoming concentration camp prisoners were stored, and "Mexico" referred to a comparably poor area of camp; "Muslim" meant a starving prisoner whose body had begun to digest itself; "to sardine" became a verb referring to stacking the murdered strategically in mass graves; and "Joy Division" signified groupings of women who were made prostitutes for Nazi staff and privileged inmates. Consequently, The Holocaust's casualties were victimized twice by words: once, when they faced cruelties they could not process mentally because they lacked the words with which to process them, and a second time, when such processing was afforded only through demeaning Nazi vocabulary. Then again, too many words may exist with which to describe something, and mental processing is then muddied, and perhaps intentionally.

As a writing professor, I have stood at the head of sizeable classrooms for almost two decades, and overhearing the conversations of the students settling in to class, I have learned something of changing student socialization and life by taking note of shifting vocabularies. It is not often I hear once-common words, such as "boyfriend," "girlfriend," and "dating." Rather, I hear now "bae" (having replaced "boo," and, like "shorty," roughly equivalent to 'a special someone,' but not necessarily the same as boyfriend or girlfriend), "friend" (someone whom one may be visiting for the purpose of emotionally and physical intimacies, frequently or infrequently), "main" (a romantic partner of first importance), "side" (a romantic partner of second or third importance, depending on how many partners one has), and "wifey" (a long-term female romantic partner, but without a state of being engaged implied). As for dating, the words are equally ambiguous: two (or more) people may be "talking to" (or seeing) each other informally, or "kicking it" or "hanging out," both of the latter verb phrases for relations far more informal than what the non-specific 'talking to' suggests already. At any rate, my students hold, in any of these relationships, one is not to "catch feelings" (become attached emotionally), lest one be seen as "thirsty" (lonely or emotionally needy); according to my students, because there is a good chance they would be cheated on by a declared boyfriend or girlfriend, it is better to avoid going steady altogether, but it is nevertheless wise to have a 'side' if one is to have a 'main' as a necessary means of pre-emptive revenge.

I include these examples, as I have done in giving the preceding Holocaust-related examples, as a way of showing how people, when attempting to describe or give shape to an **assumed material reality** with words, they can often fragment that reality and preexisting realities. What, for example, is implied when youth today fix words associated traditionally with caution, distrust, and infidelity around romance (instead of the older ideas of faith, hope, and love)? First, love is presented as a naïve illusion, and because the human psyche will internalize repeated words and their meanings quite readily, many budding, and otherwise innocent, romances will be doomed before they can even start. Thus, again, adopted language can do unintended and intended violence. Postmodernism reminds us, to be good citizens and equally good researchers, we must understand our vocabularies we learn and adapt, promote or dismiss, are not above suspicion.

In *Mother night*, a favorite novel of mine by Kurt Vonnegut, is found the warning, "We are what we pretend to be, so we must be careful about what we pretend to be." Here Vonnegut is stating the words we use to describe ourselves, our **subjective realities** (what we take to be our truths), and our search for the truth of those realities (our research), *will* be the agents of our delusion; we have only the critical power to choose to know how deluded we actually are. And it bears noting Vonnegut is using "we" in both the communal and individual senses of the word. For instance, history has shown how peoples, who find their present dismal and their future uncertain, will use language to inflate their personhood. Again, following Germany's economic collapse after World War I, the Nazis presented Germans to be inheritors to a race of genetically pure, blonde warriors, whose trueness allowed them to defeat Roman and Slav alike (though Hitler found himself having to suggest to his follower, Himmler that if he continued to promote investigative archeology, Himmler would find only evidence of the mud huts the ancient Germans lived in, and none of the marble castles of State-sponsored imagination). More currently, a racial segregationist group, the African-American-based Nation of Islam (NOI) puts forth the world was a veritable Eden, and all ancient technological accomplishments were black accomplishments, until a deformed, evil black scientist created and unleashed the so-called devilish white race, who will be held to account for pillaging the Earth after leaving its place of banishment,

Europe, by a massive spacecraft built in Japan and called the Mother Plane or Mothership (though Civil Rights leader Malcom X departed from Elijah Muhammad's description of the ancient world, Louis Farrakhan, X's rival, reaffirms a literal interpretation). Other self-aggrandizing beliefs exist today, too—like Americans of Mexican heritage are descendants of the Aztecs (though the Aztecs were one of dozens of tribes in Mexico, and numerically inferior to their neighbors)—like African-Americans are descendants of Egyptian pharaohs (though most people stolen from Africa and made into slaves were from West Africa, home to over 30 indigenous ethnic groups, and thousands of miles from Egypt)—like each of the island nations in The Caribbean was peopled by one of Twelve Tribes of Israel. Thus, we see many social groups, as had the Imperial Japanese who professed earlier to have originated in the Sun, do like to imagine a divine or semi-divine backstory for themselves.

One might ask oneself what is the harm of wearing an Egyptian ankh necklace, and imagining oneself a king, or referring to women in one's life as queens, especially if one lives paycheck-to-paycheck, or in a slum? And would it not go against self-empowerment if one were to remind oneself that most of humanity have been, say, goat herders, and not kings, and that one is, today, comparably as poor as a goat herder ever was, and unless the lottery comes in, one's family will not rise amongst the bulk of present and future humanity? One may state, also, because Colonialism ripped away the identities—and pasts—from so many peoples, no one has the right to turn a nose up to appropriating the best parts of the cultures belonging to a continent of origin; that it is a reminder of racial privilege to know one's family name and origin as they existed originally. After all, Malcom Little changed his name to Malcom X ("X" referring to the unknown) following his understanding that, "The real names of our people were destroyed during slavery. The last name of my forefathers was taken from them when they were brought to America and made slaves, and then the name of the slave master was given, which we refuse, we reject that name today and refuse it. I never acknowledge it whatsoever." However, X's **rhetorical move** holds an especially important **nuance**: he could not be certain of his family's last name prior to slavery, but rather than exchange 'Little' with an **idealized**, or romanticized, name from the East African Swahili language as many people of probable West African heritage in the United States do, his choice of 'X' showed him to embrace the uncertainty granted by postmodernism. To be clear, postmodernism will critique the person who, for instance, begins to wear kente cloth or a dashiki as a general or vague expression of regained African heritage—as any social performance is open to rhetorical analysis—but the elimination of an imposed identity, the last name "Little," and the transition to a non-identity, "X," placed Malcom X's new **ethos** (character, **credibility** (trustworthiness), or reputation) to a place just beyond postmodern analysis. The elimination of his last name showed the world he assumed nothing about his past; therefore, his present survival—existence—became central. His move suggested we regard the man only, and not any of the self-selected accessories and names that surround people. But on the contrary, the same cannot be said of the X-themed fashion apparel that became immensely popular from the late-1980's to roughly the mid-1990's, decades after the man's assassination. Case-in-point, by wearing the "X symbol" on baseball caps and T-shirts, the wearers hoped to stand out as followers of X's Civil Rights' message, and to, more importantly, appropriate the rhetorical meaning behind his name change (without the wearers' dropping their own last names); fashion producers and consumers took Malcom X's realization of personal anonymity and replaced it with conspicuous identity. By-the-way, the same went for slain communist leader Ernesto "Che" Guevara's iconic image, that, despite his ideology's stated disassociation with the accumulation of personal wealth, went on to make millions of dollars for American T-shirt producers capitalizing off of Guevara's public domain picture and teenage rebellion (that is, Che tees are found easily as mall stores, such as Hot Topic).

I have invested a bit of time in introducing postmodern thought to you as a way of introducing this book's larger subject, the philosophy of research. **Philosophy** is the search for truth. **Research** is the organized, deliberate exploration of collected data; these data are analyzed with the purpose of drawing an array of conclusions from them. A researcher's interpretations are then compared and contrasted to other researchers' conclusions during a period of **synthesis**, and from this fusion comes a wider, perhaps more meaningful understanding: the researcher now has a much greater sense of what was said about her subject in the past, and, of course, what is said at present, and of what might be said of the subject tomorrow. Every time an individual researches thoughtfully, knowledge may then be dismissed (but not eliminated; if an existing idea was shown now to be incorrect, yesterday's facts become today's artifacts; the state of being forgotten or lost suggests also a remembered or re-found state), substantiated (if the researcher's findings match those belonging to other researchers), or reimagined (but not discovered; the researcher comes up with a fresh understanding of information that was likely always at human disposal, but disregarded—think of the ever-present blue mold on harvested human food and the antibiotics to come from the mold only in the last century). Put simply, research shows reality, as far as human language can describe reality, to be in a constant state of flux. Like in nature, where physical matter is neither created nor destroyed (rather, the elements take on different forms from endless previous forms), research shows us reality follows a similar trajectory. Think of it this way: Today, a student eats a hamburger, which was once part of a cow. The beef is absorbed into the student by the process of digestion, the cow's carbon becoming part of the student's overall physical mass. A horsefly bites the student, digests that bit which was consumed, and is then preyed upon by a free-range chicken, which is ingested later by another student. Assuming the chicken had time to digest the horsefly fully, the burger's carbon will have taken on five forms in this one circle, but remains nevertheless the element, carbon. Now, imagine a turtle as large as the Earth; a number of the world's cultures once believed the world rested on the back of an immense, celestial turtle's back. For whatever reason (for example, imposed religious conversion following Colonization, an acceptance of modern astrological science, etc.), belief in this turtle waned until very few, if any, of a given people acknowledged or worshipped it. However, once-popular visual icons never really disappear, but will remain in the form of common and decorative symbols now largely without original meaning. Members of the current generation, perhaps feeling the growing stress of modern-day life and wanting to reconnect with the ancestral past as a kind of escape, search out this past, and find the innocent turtle image they grew up with played, in fact, a central role in their ancestor's lives. A community center in the shape of a turtle is then constructed. This second analogy suggests three things about research: 1) An idea may once have been paramount; 2) Like most other ideas, this idea will wane; and 3) The idea may then return, but in re-contextualized form.

Premise 4 Review Questions:

How can words affect assumed material reality?

Can words emphasize or minimize understanding?

To what extent are words important to a person's social prestige?

PREMISE 5

Consider alterity's role in research. **Alterity** refers firstly to otherness, the condition of being different. On the surface, there is little bad about difference or the investigation of it. Indeed, early human survival depended often on being able to identify poisonous fruits and vegetables from the nonpoisonous, and dangerous animals from the docile. One takes alterity then to be a basis for **recognition**, itself a platform for the more mature cognitive skills of analysis and synthesis. Though few Americans today have, for example, needed to master an ability to recognize venomous snakes while out walking, most are nevertheless familiar with the classic *Sesame Street* segment "One of these things is not like the other," a popular primary activity meant to teach children basic recognition skills. Notice then these same children are taught in the first years of schooling the recognition of basic shapes and colors, not only to expand vocabulary, but much more importantly to be able express difference verbally. A young child who becomes able to say why a triangle is not a circle is enabled as an older child to express how x is different than y in later math classes. This same individual, engaged perhaps in industry as an adult, is able to come up with a new, more efficient product, based on understanding the qualities of previous models of the product. Discrimination, then, is fundamental to human learning. However, in this context, **discrimination**, recognition of a difference, **bias**, opinion for or against something, and **taste**, personal liking for something, are comparatively innocent; here, a person will likely not be considered hateful because she prefers the color yellow over blue or anti-citrus if she chooses to eat pears instead or oranges.

Nevertheless, **alterity** refers secondly to **policed**, or socially enforced, otherness, the condition of being made to be seen as, or feel as, different from the social majority; "**to other**" is a postmodern term referring to the social act of defining a person, or group of people, as different in the subjective contexts of distasteful, exotic, less, strange, unclean, or unusual. This second definition of alterity has existed since humans began to form social groups, and continues today. The ancient Hebrews, for instance, provide us with two basic examples in their attempt to maintain cultural **homogeneity**, or uniformity, among their neighbors before the Hebrews vanquished them: Because some neighboring tribes had tattooed themselves, Hebrew priests declared the act unclean spiritually, and forbade their people tattoos; likewise, because some neighboring tribes' males went about un-circumcised, Hebrew priests declared male circumcision to be a unique bond with God, and mandated all Hebrew males to be circumcised. In other words, in the ancient world, body modification, or lack thereof, signified alterity's early application. My first example, tattooing, is interesting because religious laws surrounding it apply today, about 3,000 years later. As a Jewish male with tattoos, a number of Jewish cemeteries will not accept my corpse (as it would be offensive to those buried there already; numerical tattoos forced upon people entering concentration camps during the Holocaust could be seen as an exception, though, as the markings were imposed upon the inmates), some will (if special stickers are placed over my tattoos), but only a few will ask no questions. Christians are affected, too. Although some Christian sects believe The New Testament trumps The Hebrew Bible, or Old Testament (even if Leviticus is brought up by members in their refutations of Gay Marriage), other sects refer to both books equally. Thus, these latter Christians would appear to be forbidden tattoos, as well, but therein is found a conundrum: Religious tattoos are very popular in America today; has the Christian who has gotten a crucifix tattoo as a sign of his sincere faith somehow sinned 'less,' or is less 'unclean" before God?

You are probably sensing my second definition of alterity is related to **taboo**, a Polynesian concept encapsulating a mystical border separating the spiritually clean from the spiritually unclean. You would be correct. As a word in this context, 'taboo' can be a noun (for example, something not to do), used as an adjective (describing something as being forbidden), and even as a verb (to commit an infraction, both willingly or unknowingly). Jews and Moslems, alike, for example, are warned away from eating pork because it has been said the animal is disgusting to God (and thus one of many taboo animals, like shellfish). European Christians, however, rebuked such bias because as late as the Pre-Industrial Age, pigs were a favorite European family pet, brought into farm homes for both their body heat and personality. And secular Americans today love bacon so much today one can find bacon-themed calendars and bacon-scented novelty soap quite easily. Nevertheless, one social group's taboo set can be another group's rhetorical advantage. Remember, after the United States 'won' The Philippines after the Spanish-American War, the United States' Army found success in quelling the Moslem Moro population after threatening to bury dead Moro warriors in pig skins, thus making their souls abysmal to God. Further, Nazis at Auschwitz forced ultra-orthodox Jews to handle and shave women gassed immediately upon their arrival (it is taboo for them to touch the deceased, and only a husband may look upon an adult woman's uncovered hair) as a means of terrorizing;
not only were these Jewish separated from society, in their eyes—denied access to all-important atonement rituals—they saw themselves denied of access to God and hope.

You may be wondering now how the spirituality inherent to taboo and the discrimination underlying alterity's second definition lend themselves to research. The answer is comparatively simple: humans do not exist wholly in the world of reason; we are hardly as logical or **equitable** (fair-minded) as we would like to believe. We are almost superstitious in our research and examination of human life, mixing liberally actual science, **pseudo** (fake) science, and survival-inspired power grabs. Again, useful examples come to us from the modern-day college campus. Within some college-aged African American student communities, there exists an **amorphous** (loose), but nevertheless present, discussion of sorts referred to as "Team Light Skin vs. Team Dark Skin". Stated simply, it is a continuation of Slavery-Era plantation politics starting from when lighter-skinned slaves, those who were thought to possess physical features resembling Caucasian, were made to work closely with 'owners' in and around the comparative comfort of the plantation mansion, while their darker-skinned counterparts were made to work under the sun in the fields. This perceived material advantage—if a slave can be said to hold any advantage at all (did the Romans not say the worst death is better than the best slavery?)—coupled with whatever 'favor' male slave owners showed to their children resulting from house slave rape, put the lighter-skinned individual in a place of enduring suspicion within the larger black community, similar to the animosity the general prisoner holds traditionally toward the prison trustee colluding with the guards, forgetting importantly no slave had any choice of work assignment. Thus, after slavery, throughout Reconstruction and The Jim Crow-Era, and to today, because lighter skin continues to be seen as 'less offensive' to institutional white racism and in the common workplace, today's African-American students discuss openly the value of skin tone in America. **Concurrently**, or at the same time, some students put forth more ethnically African physical features are as, if not more, beautiful than genetically-mixed variations. Think of how 'natural' hair, curly hair un-straightened with harsh chemical treatments, is given great public esteem now. However, despite, and behind, the explicit positivity in such contemporary statements, as "Natural girls rock!", there is found a terrible binary.

A **binary** (known also as a **dichotomy**) is a socially popular, simplistic either/or proposition (for example, attractive/unattractive, black/white, good/bad, in good taste/in bad taste, masculine/feminine). A binary is un-taxing to an unthinking mind because like a taboo, a binary is a prepackaged mental construct that does the thinking for the individual as complex issues are reduced to either this-or-that propositions; the binary is also the mother of stereotype. Thus, to mention 'natural' explicitly is to mention 'unnatural' implicitly, and is 'unnatural' ever put in a positive light in everyday conversation? No, we know 'unnatural' tends to refer to abnormal or phony. In this binary, if an African-American woman who keeps 'natural' hair is to be praised because she has placed herself deliberately more closely to African heritage, the African-American woman born with straight hair, or one who straightens her hair because it is thought to be easier to care for when getting ready for work in the morning is characterized by natural hair proponents— knowingly or unknowingly—then as 'less' or 'suspect'. A contrary binary, the much older idea of having 'good hair' applies, also: straight, or 'good', hair believed to resemble stereotypical Caucasian, Native American, or Asian hair, or hair made to resemble
these, is held as better than its supposed opposite, 'bad,' kinky, 'nappy' hair. Other **iterations**,
repetitions, of this debate centering on 'degree of blackness' stem from the old 'paper bag test,' whereby shades of skin darker than said bag were less acceptable in 'polite society,' and skin tones lighter more acceptable. Perhaps Dr. Seuss was on to something when he wrote of Sneetches and their fluctuating affection for star-shaped birthmarks.

Throughout history, binaries have limited human understanding often to **superficial**, or shallow reasoning, and have condemned multitudes to lesser social status, if not fire and sword. It is ironic, but not surprising, this lessening of personal and group ethos has a foundation within religion, especially in those faiths with conversion of nonbelieving others as a primary goal, as the following binaries are common within religious **bigotry**, or strong prejudice: believer/nonbeliever (or /heathen, or /heretic, /apostate, or /atheist), saved/sinner, enlightened/obtuse, godly/ungodly, and again, clean/unclean. However, many **emancipatory** (freeing) social movements have had religion as a base, too. Anti-slavery protest (known generally as The Abolition Movement) in the Pre-Civil War United States resided in Northern churches, for instance, and the Civil Rights Movements during The Jim Crow Era were led often by Southern and Northern church people; the general religious counterargument to imposed difference in most cases being binaries cannot be allowed to exist as all humans are created in God's unifying image, and are, thus, equal to one another.

Today, we find an **analogous**, or similar, binary-eliminating effort in the form of a largely leaderless movement called Black Lives Matter (BLM). Publically, BLM's purpose is to **assert** (state openly) the equal worth of African-American lives by calling attention to police brutality toward men and women of color, confronting institutional racism, which allows people of color to be brutalized by a legal system populated historically mainly by, and favoring to, whites, reforming this legal system and retraining its publically accountable workers fundamentally, so African Americans have an equal chance at justice, and **redressing**, or fixing, dire social injustices inspired by slavery, carried on during The Jim Crow Era, and continuing on today. Put simply, BLM is attempting to eliminate another common binary, that of legal authority figure/civilian, whereby both police officer and citizen are now to be seen as of equal worth to society, and thus, each worthy of the full trust of the other. Rhetorically, BLM attempts to put forth black people, despite real or **perceived** (imagined) criminal record, are not to confronted by police officers with **scrutiny** (suspicion) or physical force; considering generally carrying of weapons, physical violence (hitting an officer), public intoxication (from drug use or otherwise), refusing to follow an officer's orders, or running from an officer no cause at all for lethal force; for any police officer to kill a civilian would be to act illegally, or at minimum, extra-judicially or **summarily**, without providing a citizen the constitutional benefit of official legal proceedings. Moreover, in the context of this binary's elimination, the African American is entitled to say no to a police officer as, historically, the police officer has not had his or her best interests at heart, and, after all, the police officer is merely a public servant, anyway (which is reminiscent of the Black Panthers late-1960's call to free all people of African heritage, regardless of crime, from American prisons). One wonders if this last point is the central tragedy of the Sandra Bland affair; did she, perhaps, rebuke the officer who pulled her over because she thought the world had changed after a number of race-related street protests went unstopped by police, that she believed the legal authority figure/civilian binary had been eliminated already from society as a result of these protests? Or, maybe, she fell victim to **pandering**, being indulged, by the press?

As I have mentioned earlier in this text, the press today is hardly objective. To listen to National Public Radio (NPR) now, for instance, one would assume The United States does not gravitate toward center-right politics, and 'The Silent Majority,' the bulk of citizens interested most in constancy and law and order who Republicans are fond to allude to, has vanished from the land. In a word, BLM's rhetoric continues to gain momentum because corporate and non-corporate media alike seem fearful to question the movement inasmuch two new terms, 'blandering' and 'hispandering,' meaning to pander to African-Americans and Hispanic peoples openly in the press, now exist. For news outlets, like NPR, it is seemingly enough to get 'the African American opinion' because BLM bases itself importantly also on gaining public sympathy (think of the NPR's segment, Codeswitch), enough for the radio station to leave it at that, and applaud itself for lending its airwaves to this great national 'discussion'. Meaning, as BLM attempts to draw attention away from what civilian actions and criminal history may have led to lethal police-civilian interactions, the aforementioned 'Silent Majority' does want this contextual information to be part of the discussion, now questioning aloud if people who "Live by the sword, die by the sword"; this cognitive **disjunction**, or lack of agreement, appears to be only growing. More importantly, in its attempt to remove the legal authority figure/civilian binary from social **discourse**, or conversation, BLM puts forth nevertheless a concurrent taboo: one is not to bring up the topic of black-on-black violence when speaking of violent police-civilian interactions. To do so would make the speaker appear, at best, **reactionary** (old fashioned and against the movement) or, at worst, racist; this latter term thought by the political left to be cringe worthy, as its bearer has lost all ethos by committing social suicide. Rather than interpret the militarization of policing in economically poorer areas to be a contextual result of the nearly 10,000 black men dying at the hands of other black men since the death of Treyvon Martin a few years ago (almost one-fifth the number of people America lost during the Vietnam War), BLM considers the **premise**, or idea, to be a **strawman**, a smoke screen, because legal systems can be fixed and overseen by the public, but street gangs cannot.

Perhaps the most **inscrutable**, or difficult-to-understand, anti-alterity movement, though, is found in the current redefinition of the 'safe space' and its newly **concomitant**, or associated, 'trigger warnings'. Historically, the safe place on college campuses were offices of progressive faculty and staff where people could escape the all-too-real dangers presented by homophobia; these faculty and staff acting, then, as **advocates**, or supporters, for gay, lesbian, bisexual, and transgendered peoples, and working toward ending the **cynicism**, or negativity, associated with another binary, that of straight/gay. Since at least 2010, the safe place was meant also to shelter bullied students, taking on, then, the alpha-individual/zeta-individual (most socially dominant person/least socially dominant person) binary. In the past year, however, the safe space has been redefined to be both 'judgement-free' and 'stress-free' zones as well. In other words, the safe space is tasked contradictorily now with taking on all binaries a student may feel oppressed by, and, at the same time, ignoring, so as not to offend, whatever binaries the student considers essential to his or her core values. Thus, while working in a safe space, one may find oneself encouraging students to employ their freedom of speech, but if a public counterargument to their point of view makes these students 'uncomfortable,' one is to help these students **suppress**, or limit, the freedom of speech of others; judgement-free, refers, then, more to judgement redirected, and less to judgement eliminated. And thus, the student advocate becomes a fascist censor of sorts: Even if a student was to find himself or herself in a class that encourages all viewpoints without exception, that student would, nevertheless, be justified today to report a professor to a student advocate simply because the professor presents opposing points of view to be equal to the student's beliefs. At minimum, the professor would be seen then as suspect by the school, and at worst, the professor may lose his or her position because one student did not feel his or her belief was **substantiated**, or validated, fully. However, the historical point of university is to challenge all preexisting assumptions, though these assumptions may be comfortable; the worth of research is found directly in the research's originality, though originality is taken often to be code for uncomfortable radicalism. In this way, today's safe place appears to **run counter**, or go against, the mission of education and its basis, research, because it puts forth subjective **dogma**, creed or belief, is superior to objective analysis.

Not helping matters is the publicized appearance of university administrations caving-in so easily to current student demands, in their important efforts to maintain equity and the financial bottom line, student enrollment. Not that all student demands are frivolous; that is hardly the case. Still, the aforementioned trigger warning bears significant analysis. Today, many professors are asked by their administrators to include trigger warnings, disclosures of possibly unpleasant content, on their syllabi to avoid prompting post-traumatic stress disorder (PTSD) episodes, offending students, and provoking campus equity investigations and student protests. These trigger warnings are placed often on the most basic and mainstream of classes, for example: African American studies (because slavery was cruel), anthropology (because the values held by the world's peoples may be different from the students') biology (because evolution may be mentioned), composition (because students will be expected to consider counterarguments to their claims), history (because wars are violent), literature (because the works of past authors may reflect the now-unfashionable values of the authors' times), Holocaust studies (because genocide is sad), physical science (because global warming may be mentioned), political science (because a number of terrorists today self-describe as Moslem, and because undocumented migration is defined still as illegal), sociology (because peoples' economic class, race, and social privilege may be mentioned), world religions (because other people believe in other gods), etc. Each of these cautions suggest American students today are generally sheltered, but more importantly, that they tend not to see their values questioned off of campus; thus, when on campus, being shown a diversity of thoughts can be interpreted as a devastating series of **existential**, or being-based, threats.

As a writing professor, I am interested greatly in student open-mindedness because it is my job to position students to be leaders in their respective fields through the mastery of original, thought-provoking writing. What does it mean, then, to the future of research if many of these students appear unwilling to challenge their initial beliefs of themselves, others, and the world? Now, if one is to believe the praise given to the millennial generation in the media and at college orientation pep talks, which holds the world has never before seen a generation so accepting of others, one could be missing an essential point: Social **fragmentation**, or break up, does not equal **social cohesion**, or unity. Yes, that old schoolyard binary, jock/nerd, appears to have gone the way of the dinosaur, but its possible extinction has less to do with a new level of respect for fellow humans, and more to do with a growing taste for ignoring the person next to us. The
current 'You do you, and I'll do me' slogan is based specifically on a new social contract, 'Do as you like as long as it does not affect me,' itself based on the older, defensive plea, 'You don't know me. You can't judge me,' and the even older statement, 'I have my own truth.' Put simply, passive, unlearned tolerance has overtaken active, learned acceptance as a social **paradigm**, or model, because tolerance is far less mentally straining for people than acceptance is; having no questions for someone leads to needing no answers from someone. Consider, for example, the loss some feminists find themselves at when discussing female genital mutilation (FMG), a topic common in anthropology, sociology, and women's studies courses. On the one hand, feminists, in general, believe questioning the values expressed by another culture is distinctly chauvinist because questioning and judgement come often from a place of self-entitlement, or privilege. On the other hand, since

most feminists see FMG as distinctly anti-woman, as it is a surgical way males of some cultural groups in Africa and the Near East attempt to control the lives of women physically, the **notion**, or idea, of academic hypocrisy tends to be wrestled with when discussing FMG. Therefore, a misplaced sense of shame can be said to be **imparted**, or given, to academic work: People who have learned to tolerate all difference are put at ill-ease when they are made to confront differing value judgements. Further, and confusing this paradigm, there are, on campuses, those students who call for varying levels of tolerance. Gay Rights, for instance, are said by some students not to be equal to Civil Rights because one can be gay and 'in the closest,' or hidden safely from society, but one cannot not be black and in the closet; blackness is granted no pass in a racist society, so African Americans are to be given more legal protections. Similarly, a T-shirt popular when I was an undergraduate, which said, "It's a Black thing. You wouldn't understand," and today's version, which states, "Unapologetically Black" both suggest to tolerate cultural difference is all non-blacks are allowed to do because to accept implies conscious judgement on the part of ethnic others. One manner of policing this imposed limitation to tolerance some students take today is the public citing of **inferred**, or assumed, 'micro-aggressions,' subtle or implied words or actions made against members of a minority group.

Interestingly, the anti-alterity call to tolerate can make a professor's evaluation of student writing a comparatively more difficult, and almost political, task. A research paper is, at heart, the studied arrangement and **synthesis**, or fusion, of ideas collected from many scholars, including— fundamentally —a student's own ideas. The student's paper is graded, then, on the expansiveness of her research; the more complexity of ideas, or thoroughness, the student demonstrates in her writing, the higher her paper's grade will be. Moreover, historically, the professor has expected the student to put forth not only research favorable to her opinion, but to consider, also, and at much length, research unfavorable to her opinion and to **reconcile**, or resolve, it by paper's end; therefore, objectivity has held an important place in the writing process, and is related to paper grade, as well. That said, a paper to have put forth only the student's opinion would be seen by the professor, at best, as one-sided, or at worst, as a rant. But what of the student who has little intention to be objective in her research and writing because she is certain of the **veracity**, or accuracy, of her own truth? What is the quality of this person's researched work? In my time as a writing professor, I have encountered each of the following challenges: 1) A number of students will cite only the Christian Bible, regardless of the class' theme, because they consider it unquestionably perfect in content and the only book they will ever need; 2) Other students holding to racist viewpoints will cite only Internet sources putting forth the same worldviews because the traditional press is thought to be corrupted and, thus, untrustworthy; 3) Students, who have become conspiracy-minded, like many people will do around a turn of a century, will depend upon television and radio shows and other 'nontraditional' media; and 4) Yet more students will adhere simply to a party line and **parrot**, or mimic, a political platform.

Just ten years ago none of these challenges would have been too difficult. A note to "revise and resubmit" written at the end of a paper would have been more than enough to encourage a student to address the needs of rigorous college-level research more actively. Today is different, though. That pop news programs, such as *Good Morning America*, talk of authors finding their own truths suggests art imitates life inasmuch truth is seen by many of the
public as singular, or limited to the individual, and not multiple, or many sided. And because mass media promote readily the sides of stories their audiences agree with already, it is not surprising some students take one-sidedness to be the

unquestioned norm. Therefore, if, today, I was to instruct a student to move beyond using the Bible exclusively in her research for the sake of thoroughness, she may take my advice as beneficial to her writing, she may ignore my advice altogether, or she may see it as an attack on her person and on her faith, and cite me as anti-Christian. Once, in a moment of humor, an assistant of mine, an evangelical Christian, pulled from her book bag a pamphlet she received from her recent Christian summer camp entitled, "How to survive your ungodly English professor" to our mutual laughter. Further, I have been called a "race traitor" by students affiliated with white supremacist movements, not knowing I am Jewish (had they known, I would have been called a "race enemy," instead), when I questioned the Internet-only research behind their discussions of the so-called sacred purity of white blood, and I was called "white devil" by black supremacists as I questioned their Internet-only research of the so-called spiritual divinity of black women, genetic superiority of black men, and Jewish control of world finance and politics. Though in the second and third cases above, as a professor, I am not worried about being hauled before a campus equity board for questioning racist thinking—provided I do not call racists, racist (campus administrations warn professors from doing so as the term is offensive to self-described bigots)—I am, however, troubled a segment of the student population has convinced itself that research drawn from traditional or mainstream publishing houses can provide few meaningful data. Bigots, both black and white, tend to view publishing as an industry corrupted by (in the imagination of white supremacists) a politically liberal Jewish elite bent on diluting the aforementioned white blood through its encouragement of multicultural diversity, and by (in the imagination of black supremacists) a politically conservative Jewish elite bent on obscuring the magnificence of a black Ancient Egypt and African contributions to the world, profiteering during black suffering, and lifting up and

bringing down, when convenient, black leaders (think of the growing conversation suggesting Bill Cosby's fall from grace was not the result of being accused of sexual assault by a number of women, but because he, an African American male, sought to purchase the NBC television network). Further still, and though less worrisome than research limited by racial prerogative, but perplexing nonetheless, is the research of those students, for whom conspiracy theories found on the Internet hold as much weight as anything found in a juried research article. Again, as with the value granted to one-sided thinking today, students are not wholly to blame; most Americans have heard the Internet described as the "Information Superhighway," where answers to many of life's questions can be found easily. And, increasingly, in high schools, tomorrow's college students perform research through the Web almost exclusively. Thus, while some **conjecture** (speculation)-laden student research is merely the result of juvenile curiosity for the forbidden exotic (I am thinking of the popular campus notion some years back that held human evolution was started by the great apes consuming psychedelic mushrooms), much of it reproduces merely in a roundabout way the continual human fear of the unknown; think of the Dark Ages' 'demon,' yesterday's 'New World Order' (NWO), and today's 'alien,' 'Freemason,' and 'Illuminati'—all the same boogeyman discussed at length online. Some of it appears, though, to demonstrate superstition is alive-and-well in America (one may be surprised at the number of students who wish to argue Satan is at work
during periods of bad weather, but my question, "Will you be interviewing him?" tends to prompt subject changes), and some it appears, also, to suggest the work of mentally-troubled minds, the border between conspiratorial and schizophrenia-inspired writing a narrow one frequently. Much more common, however, is student research which simply tows a political line: politically liberal students will

tend to favor liberal theorists exclusively, and politically conservative students will tend to favor conservative theorists exclusively; a professor, then, who calls forth an opinion other than a liberal one in class runs the risk of being seen by the liberals as a sellout, or, if the professor does not refer to a conservative point of view, as the embodiment of the liberal professor stereotype. Here students are just mimicking the gridlock they see in American politics.

Premise 5 Review Questions:

How would postmodernism respond to Premise 5?

Which social binaries, if any, shape how you see the world? Do other people's social binaries attempt to shape you? If so, how?

To what extent does personal ego affect student research?

PREMISE 6

   Pathos is a concept taken from Ancient Greek education referring to the kinds of emotions applied by a speaker or writer to a discussion, the feelings these emotions create within a discussion's audience, and the level of passion the speaker or writer works with. I have mentioned earlier in this book the English language makes use of this concept in two of its common verbs, to sympathize and to empathize. Again, to sympathize means to find common feeling through open-minded imagination, as in "I haven't experienced this situation myself, but yes, that must be frustrating," and to empathize means to find common feeling through shared experience, as in "Wow, I know what that's like". Though to empathize is thought to be a stronger idea because it reflects a specific social connection, to sympathize is considered nevertheless an important stepping stone to social connection. Moreover, *pathos* is thought to be an essential tool when writing for the humanities and social sciences because both fields center themselves around human concern; without **engendering**, or creating, sympathy or empathy for the people discussed in such a paper, it is believed the writer is writing merely to please herself, and is not fulfilling her central task, to improve the lives or understanding of others. On the contrary, *pathos* does not possess the same level of respect in writing centered on the physical sciences because, there, a paper's topic, research method, and findings are thought to be, or should be, exciting enough in of themselves, and any addition of human emotion into writing is to be seen as fluff clouding **neutral**, or unbiased, scientific logic and data analysis.

Logos is another concept taken from Ancient Greek education, and is a bit more abstract than *pathos*. It refers to word and word choice (inasmuch a word is a basic unit of thought, like an inch is a basic unit of measurement), text (in both a physical form, like a book, but also, and importantly, in a nonphysical, psychological form, like a cultural **schema**, or script—that is to say, learned knowledge of what to expect and do in a given situation, like a holiday), and reason, in the context of logic. To employ logic when writing is to choose the most meaningful words, to arrange these words in the most **efficient**, or well-organized, manner, and to outline the progression of ideas according to the specific expectations of the writing's **genre**, or type. Writing logically is thought today, moreover, to be a brain-based activity, and hence popular with scientists (as writing with *pathos* is thought be based in the heart, and hence popular with humanists), but the Ancient Greeks saw no such binary here; rather, they saw *logos*, *pathos*, and *ethos* (again, an author's reputation) as necessary, equal concepts within any speech or writing. In other words, the Ancient Greeks held a composition is most successful if it appeals to an audience's mind (because its language and facts are precise and organized well), if it strikes the audience's heart (because humans are emotional beings, who like stimulation), and if it is composed by someone trustworthy. And though most writing professors encourage this three-pronged approach (referred to often as **Aristotle's Triangle**) in their classrooms, the world outside the campus does not always promote the same. Facts, it seems, are thought sometimes to get in the way of spirit.

We must ask ourselves if we live in another Romantic age. To be clear, 'Capital R'-Romantic speaks of Romanticism, a vast social movement stressing inspiration, imagination, and personal subjectivity, which displaced the logic-based Age of Reason in the late-1700s, succumbed to Modernism, another logic-based social movement, by the mid-1800's, and reappeared briefly in the late 1960s, lending shape to artistic, Civil Rights, and anti-Vietnam War movements. Most social protests tend to be Romantic, imagining as they do often radically new social realities; "revolution," means, after all, a turnaround. However, the initial **impetus**, or motivation, behind most social protests is logic—remember, the first Civil Rights' protest signs said simply, "I am a man". Nevertheless, it appears, for a protest to become a movement, and for that movement to become what German theorists call a *zeitgeist,* or spirit of the times, something more than logic is required; a population will need to become impassioned.

It is apparent discussion of race has become a *zeitgeist*. I am still processing a suggestion Brendan Kiely, co-author of a new race-based novel, *All American boys*, made during a National Public Radio (NPR) interview. He suggested, when considering race, people ought to think less logically and more empathetically. Though he spoke from a place of liberal politics, his idea crosses many racial movements. I, for example, have seldom met a racist, black or white, who spoke of hating anybody, them saying instead, "We do not hate *x people*, but we love *y people*". This common expression makes a conscious nod toward logic (because most of the public will take hate to be illogical), while it centralizes, knowingly, the idea of love, also. The irony of self-described racial supremacists talking about love aside, love creates strong *pathos*, and it is a smart rhetorical move to capitalize on it. Social scientists, after all, are quick to point to Maslow's idea that love is central to sustaining human life in his Hierarchy of Needs principle. The public, then, is to turn on to emotion almost wholly, and to see a disregard of logic not so much as a turning off of conscious thought, but as a kind of Romantic liberation from existing thought. Consider a dispute Black Lives Matter (BLM) has with a more amorphous group, All Lives Matter (ALM): Again, BLM was founded to draw singular attention to the worth of black lives in the face of perceived legal and economic repression. ALM, on the other hand, asserts disasters befalling one people are no less tragic when they happen to other peoples. Consider then the general BLM response to ALM manifested across social media: 'Look, we believe all peoples to be equal, but we are the ones suffering now, so we choose to focus only on us, and you should, too, okay?' In a word, BLM recommends Americans stop, at least for now, from thinking of society as a whole, and to, instead, limit their thought to stated Afro-centric concern. Moreover, BLM suggests, ALM's decision to focus on social multiplicity is a result of a conscious, white-inspired, and perhaps racist, decision to **sublimate**, or channel important attention away from, the black experience, denying, thus, BLM's call for **uncritical**, or unquestioned, empathy.

I recall watching a news program covering a police shooting-related street protest, which filmed a crying African-American woman, who was saying, "We just want to be understood". I took her spoken plea to come from a genuine place, considering the earnestness of her body language; after setting her heel, she did not speak to the camera, but rather to the protest's onlookers. I wondered, however, if the protest's onlookers and news program's viewers took her words to be a call for sympathy or empathy. I wondered, further, if she, herself, knew which. Were it a call for sympathy, it would be a request for her audiences to displace their own lived realities for a moment, and to imagine the fear that is said to come with being young, black, poor, and even a motorist of color, in America today— Remember, a person who is able to imagine another person's suffering is less likely to be a perpetrator of future suffering. In this way, sympathy is taken to be less intrusive to cognitive thought because 'walking a mile in another person's shoes' is believed more by people to be a reminder to act with the feelings of others in mind; sympathy allows for multiple thoughts. But what if her statement was an encompassing call for empathy, for her culturally diverse audiences to find a singular unity with the people she was protesting for?

Again, to empathize means to find common feeling through shared lived experience. This definition assumes, of course, beyond our knowledge that each human is genetically *homo sapiens*, belonging to the same human animal family, shared lived experience may be found among peoples with radically different social backgrounds. It is here **contemporary**, or current, uses of empathy call perhaps for a suspension of disbelief; that is to say, logical social comparisons should be ignored by peoples who are asked to be empathetic. We are forced, then, to ask ourselves if empathy affects the level of intellectual honesty in research; if any unflattering facts are to be put to the side in the manner of open, but undiscussed, secrets for the sake of being compassionate or nice. This question becomes **salient**, or pronounced, especially when one finds oneself having to refer to a wide political spectrum of sources in an attempt to study the latest police-civilian violence fully. When the aforementioned woman told us "We just want to be understood," she could have been implying we are to mourn the dead, *despite* the general understanding that the lives of people with long criminal records, or those who confront police physically, or those who sell, or are dependent on, hard drugs end badly often; that we are to understand, also, each of these people was someone's son or daughter, as are we. Thus, we are not to smirk or shake our heads condescendingly when during the now-inevitable interview with the deceased's parents, the mother or father tells the camera his or her child was a good boy or girl. As importantly, the woman could have taken understanding to mean the problems within her economically-depressed community are, in actuality, the problems of most every American community.

Empathy calls on people to resist saying "I have nothing in common with you". This is a tall proposition for many people, considering it defies the immediate recognition of observed subjective reality; differences in life experiences can, after all, be noted without much effort. In the context of discussion of race today, most Americans have not served time in prison (though more often than not African-American males are said to be imprisoned in numbers disproportionate to other ethnic groups), most Americans have not sold drugs (which is not to say many of this majority have not bought or used illegal drugs, they have; rather, people living in economically-depressed areas may see drug dealing as an infinitely practical enterprise—the fewer jobs available, the greater demand for chemical mental escape), most Americans have graduated high school and are literate (though graduation rates in many urban high schools can range today between 25- and 60-percent), and most Americans did not become parents in their teen-age years (though teen-age birth rates among all ethnicities have been decreasing nationally). In short, it can be supposed most Americans possess at least a basic level of hope for the future because they believe themselves to have survived the system; for example, this majority probably views law enforcement as necessary to maintaining social *decorum*, or dignity, earned during the course of life. On the contrary, if many of a person's friends and family were imprisoned, and he feared being imprisoned himself, if he faced chronic unemployment and was persuaded to believe the selling of illegal drugs was the only way to make it, if his chances for social advancement were limited because he never graduated high school, and if he found himself having to provide for children before he was 18-years-old, this person may take the view his future is hopeless, and that law enforcement is, collectively, a guardian set against people like him. One should not be surprised, then, some opponents to BLM will put forth public criticisms, such as 'Do not break the law if you do not want an altercation with the police' or 'do not sell drugs if you do not want to go to jail' because acting outside of the law makes little sense to people who take what they consider to be their experience, an orderly life, to be the **apex**, or height, of civilization. Neither should one be surprised when BLM speaks of cultural survival—African-Americans make up only about 13.5-percent of the nation's population, and the conservative Jim Crow legislation and segregation of past years, combined with the liberal War on Poverty's preference for assigning more financial assistance to single mothers than intact families, was uniquely successful in devastating a people reeling already from centuries of slavery. Thus the researcher, in her attempt to analyze social discourse, may be seen as a gadfly, an irritating busybody, by the comfortable majority if she were to suggest desperate people will tend to act desperately, and they deserve forgiveness for rioting and burning property, or that their learned sense of entitlement rests on the back of a disenfranchised people; that today's generations are, largely unknowingly, benefitting materially from the cultural exploitation led by their ancestors or culture's members. And thus, the researcher may be seen as a scold and bigot by people favorable to BLM if she were to

suggest, through data, a fellow black male is more dangerous to another black male than the police are, that more white males have died in altercations with police than black males have, and that the many thousands of deaths as a result of 'black-on-black' crime is a problem perhaps more demanding to the community than zealous law enforcement. Most importantly, the researcher must defy heavy social pressures, placed often in the name of assigning empathy, to ignore one data set or another
if she wishes to present the truth wholly and with as little bias as possible.

Beyond race, conversation regarding empathy extends to politics. For example, the presidential candidacy of Hillary Clinton has been framed in media as groundbreaking because she is an especially successful female politician in a male-dominated political world, but more specifically, her success as a woman has become symbolic to many of her female followers, who describe Clinton's rise as being felt evidence that today is 'our time,' the **fruition**, or fulfillment, of decades-long Second Wave feminist struggle for gender equality. Descriptions of Clinton's ascendancy take on, then, a distinctly early-1970's flavor, reminiscent of the classic Virginia Slims' cigarette ad campaign of that era, which told newly liberated women entering the white collar workforce for the first time, "You've come a long way, Baby". The logical argument behind women's entrance into professional workplaces, concurrent with, and similar to, feminist protests for the Equal Rights Amendment (ERA), proposed the reproductive organs one has neither increases nor decreases one's value as a worker; a woman can handle a job as well as a man, and she ought to be paid the same wages her male counterpart receives. However, despite Clinton, like most her supporters, having benefitted from the continuing elimination of gender as a criterion for worthiness, that many women interviewed by the press during campaign coverage say they will vote for Clinton because she is female, like them, as often as they say she is the most qualified candidate, suggests the aforementioned logical argument of the early 1970's against gender discrimination may have given way to a more gender-driven *zeitgeist*. A feeling of female oneness has, perhaps, overshadowed the logic of human unity.

Lastly, empathy is discussed today in terms of degree, with descriptive word choice presented as an essential window to the level of compassion different social groups hold for one another. German legal authorities do not, for instance, dispute the fact hundreds of women were assaulted sexually by men of Middle Eastern and North African descent in Cologne, Germany on December 31, 2015, New Year's Eve; rather, how best to describe these men and their alleged crimes has been the subject of much anxiety for the world's progressive, or liberal, press. Put simply, if this press was to empathize with the assaults' survivors openly (think of the massive attention the same press brought to sexual assault and survivor's rights on American college campuses over the past years), and described them as victims, the inevitable question of whom these women were victim to would be brought up. And if the men pointed to happen to belong to ethnic minorities, or are part of a threatened population fleeing war in a vast migration, or belong to a misunderstood religion, as Islam is described by media often, then the progressive press would find itself addressing its basic platform, that most difference among humans is simply a matter of unenlightened misunderstanding. Thus, in its anxious determination to provide understanding for somebody, the press felt itself limited to being either 1) pro-women and unnecessarily judgmental toward the cultural groups the alleged perpetrators belong to (though German legal authorities believe upwards of one-thousand Muslim men were involved, advocates for the men remind us the world is home to over a billion Muslims, so one-thousand forms an almost insignificant percentage), or 2) being culturally sensitive to a generalized conservative Muslim male point of view and dismissing the sexual assaults as evidence that even today's notably socially-liberal Europe is still home to sexism, and these men were merely mimicking observed sexist European behaviors (though German legal authorities believe the attacks were planned, the advocates describe the attacks more as spontaneous outbursts by a newly emigrated, **patriarchal** (male-led), and perhaps sexually-repressed, male populace seeking to punish women, and by extension, a sex-positive, or sexually liberal, Europe. By-and-large, the progressive press sought to understand the men more, suggesting questioning of the men's alleged behavior was a form of victim blaming: an outnumbered ethnic other is in dangerous social, legal, and economic positions already. The mainstream press tended to avoid serious discussion of the subject altogether, having dedicated a minute or two to the story as a general news item.

We see discussion of additional empathetic describers in further arenas, such as social protest and petty crime. People who take a cause to the street are referred to commonly as protesters, and if they abide by the law while on the street expressing themselves, as it is their constitutional right to do so, they are thought of moreover as peaceful protesters. However, questions shared by the political left and right arise if property is damaged or destroyed during the protest—Has this protest become a riot, and have the protesters become rioters? And if the protest to have become violent involved many people, should effort be made by the press, with objectivity in mind, to describe those people demonstrating as belonging to two separate groups, peaceful protesters and rioters? Rhetorically, the difference between "peaceful protester" and "rioter" is significant. Peaceful protest is not only protected by The Constitution, but given Thomas Jefferson called on each generation to rebel, to protest is thought by some as a naturally American thing to do, and protesters as true American patriots. Rioting, on the other hand, may grant police immediate extra-judicial powers against a movement because such a street action is thought by many as mob, or unthinking, violence, though a few may excuse riotous behavior as an irrational, but nevertheless human expression (as in crime of passion). Thus, social movements strive to have its members be seen by the public as easy-to-empathize-with patriots, and not as lawbreakers, who the general public cannot relate to; in this way, the non-violent social movements led by Mahatma Gandhi and Martin Luther King, Jr., are held commonly as almost perfect examples of responsible protest while more leaderless movements, such as Occupy and Black Lives Matter (BLM) have been dogged by recorded images of broken windows and burning cars and buildings (though on social media, BLM members will state sometimes the time for passive resistant is over, and the time for direct action has begun). Further still, newer questions ask, what is the value difference in name between a "militia" and a "terrorist organization" (having the old saying, "One man's terrorist is another man's freedom fighter" in mind) if both take up arms to affect political change, and who decides which group is which? Another question, what to call a person who has committed a crime, has appeared, also. Oakland, California's Center for Media Justice, for instance, has recommended San Francisco Bay Area residents avoid "shaming" law breakers; one, for example, is not to call a person who stole one's bicycle a "thief" because that would be embarrassing and offensive; rather, one should describe the individual as "the person who stole my bike".

Premise 6 Review Questions:

Why do some people have difficulty joining heart and head when researching?

How prevalent are Romantic ideals on your campus?

In the context of protesting, what does "peace" mean in the legal charge of "Disturbing the peace"?

PREMISE 7

There are said to be two principal methods of research today, **qualitative** (descriptive) and **quantitative** (statistical), though because dozens of qualitative sub-methods exist now, cross-pollination between the qualitative and quantitative is increasingly more common. Qualitative research tends to be dependent upon 'deep reading,' known also as **meta-analysis**, insofar this method is interested most in exploring an observed event's all-important context, collecting past and present scholarly interpretations of the specific event and similar events, and analyzing the subjective inspiration behind the researcher's work, itself. Qualitative studies tend also to be **discrete**, or limited, as a result of the depth they hope to attain; work in this vein prefers small sample sizes because long-term, open-ended interviews with research volunteers are thought to provide much fuller pictures than the generalized data anonymous surveys can provide. Further, given the closeness of researcher and research volunteer in this work, qualitative researchers embed themselves often within the communities they are studying, and it is from qualitative research that we have learned for a researcher studying people to be most effective, she must be fluent in the language or dialect spoken by those she is studying (employing a translator can only skew meaning). Historically, qualitative research has provided us with a library of ideas, which may be transformed later into hypotheses when studies' research samples are joined together to form **representative**, or valid, population percentages.

On the other hand, quantitative research is math based. Unlike qualitative research, it hopes to transform data collected from many people into statistics, from which

general meanings and patterns are then drawn. And its primary instrument is the survey, not the interview. In a word, it is the goal of any quantitative study to capture the opinions of, at minimum, at least 10-percent of a studied population as a means of ensuring so-called study **validity**, or legitimacy. It is important also to quantitative research that the researcher maintain her objectivity, that the questions chosen for a survey reflect the needs of the study specifically, and not her subjective interest. In fact, in quantitative research's most orthodox, or purest, form, most any interaction between researcher and research volunteers is seen as capable of influencing volunteers to answer survey questions the way they think the researcher wants them to (we refer to this as **The Hawthorne Effect**); thus, surveys tend to be distributed as anonymously as possible through the Web, the mail, and if absolutely needed to, by an assistant to the researcher. Moreover, just as a survey is seen as a research instrument, so is the researcher; if a survey is said to contain **measures** (questions), the researcher is said to be a processor of the raw data that the answers to the questions may contain. Lastly, because quantitative research is a much older method than the qualitative, and given its objective, facts-only emphasis, it is seen by its proponents, and many publishing houses, as more logical than other research methods; quantitative research is thought to be a lasting expression of **empirical**, or experiential, research while qualitative research is held to be a home to the biased opinions of a few. Nevertheless, I maintain while quantitative analysis may, for instance, tell us the number of teen mothers in a given neighborhood, and that nonuse of birth control was a variable, in talking to these young women, qualitative analysis may
tell us why they, themselves, became pregnant.

Stereotypes surround both qualitative and quantitative research methods. I have suggested already qualitative research is criticized for its comparatively small sample sizes, but more important to the method's critics is the active, pronounced role the researcher can take within this work; little consideration is said to be given in placing need for a study over the researcher's interest in the subject. That is to say, a researcher more inclined to social activism tends to employ the qualitative method. Is, for example, the researcher putting forth work to increase the world's body of knowledge neutrally, or is she seeking to add to a political position? And is research with a political bent scientific exploration or is it public propaganda? One source of this stereotype is derived from the era it sprung from largely, the politically radical 1960's, though the method's earliest incarnations can be just as easily be said to have been in the Early-Twentieth Century anthropological work of Malinowski and Evans-Pritchard; that the two men thought to live in the homelands (Micronesia; Upper-Central East Africa, respectively) of the peoples they studied, and to depend upon the opinions of those peoples more, and on the opinions of colonial administrators less, was considered truly revolutionary. Thus, because qualitative research makes its research volunteers authorities on their own experiences, and may depend less on the opinions of established academic experts, qualitative work is characterized sometimes as 'feel good' and amateurish.

Conversely, quantitative research has been described by its detractors as cold, **devoid** (lacking) of context, unsympathetic, and even fascist. Each of these criticisms appear to have come from this research method's single-minded preference for statistics: Can, for instance, something as abstract as emotional human life be described with abstract symbols, such as numbers? Are numbers able to provide the explanations of a study's data the researcher, herself, is uncomfortable providing us with lest her neutrality be put into question by her peers? Will humans, who are divided into percentages be more or less likely to recognize the shared humanity of all after learning where they have been placed? May statistics be used to maintain institutional racism and sexism? Because the development of the quantitative research method coincided with the birth of The Industrial Revolution, the method is associated with not only the benign (the formation of pathology (the study of disease) and the rise of medicine, for example), but also with the malign (eugenics, Nazism, and Jim Crow Segregation, for instance); therefore, as a research method, quantitative work is thought by some to be suspect, that statistical data may be manipulated to suit whatever *zeitgeist*, positive or negative, may be currently at play. Moreover, correctly or incorrectly, quantitative research has been stereotyped further as being an utterly male enterprise insofar as historically male-dominated academic departments and scientific foundations left to manage their own hiring committees have tended to repopulate themselves with the selection of people most similar to themselves—other males. Thus, the public face of 'the expert,' as far as quantitative research has been considered the home to scientific expertise, continues to be the male face, so much so that even women entering the sciences today are described often as feminist pioneers challenging traditional social power structures openly. A further stereotype, the 'male know-it-all' stems from this public face. Consider the currently popular slang term, "mansplaining," as when a man, thinking himself more informed or logical than women, butts into a conversation among females to offer, perhaps, redundant information or unneeded explanation.

Beyond the stereotypes caricaturing the two research methods is a frequent cognitive mistake made by casual observers from among the general public, the confusion of imagined data for actual data. A researcher employing the qualitative method knows, for instance, when she is studying a Native American family belonging to a particular tribe, those research volunteers can speak only for their own experiences with, and understandings of, their tribe; the researcher neither believes, nor does she imagine, this one family can speak for all of the tribe's families. Put simply, she understands an individual is merely one of many expressions of a social group, and an individual cannot be the definition of a social group. However, a person interested in the tribe may pick up the researcher's article or book, and if this person is not versed in qualitative research, and ignores the researcher's underlying context, the reader may believe, genuinely, a full understanding of the tribe has now been gained. Fear of this common mistake among public readership is found throughout qualitative work. We recall writer Hunter S. Thompson held this worry so much that within the first pages of his popular **ethnography**, or cultural study, *The Hells Angels: A strange and terrible saga*, he reminds the reader not to go looking for the motorcyclists described in his study, that the people he studied, in a way, exist no longer. For one, he wrote of the motorcycle club's founding Oakland, California chapter as they existed specifically in the Mid-1960's; the clubmen were different before he embedded himself with them because they existed prior without whatever influence his outsider's presence brought. Without an outside observer watching them, Oakland's Hells Angels just were; there was little need to take the array of Hell Angels' personas beyond the diverse rebellious social performances the spectrum of their identity held open to the members already. In a word, there was previously no need to explain and sell their lifestyle to Thompson or to 'show off' further otherwise. Next, given publication of Thompson's book coincided with immense media and public interest in outlaw motorcycle clubs, he sensed Oakland's Hells Angels would never again be the same as he found them originally: Understanding full well most of the public would take their self-descriptions of biker life without question (though the Hells Angels, themselves, believed their worldview represented, at most, one-percent of all bikers, and even referred to themselves as "1%er's"), this founding chapter intended to capitalize on the national attention they were receiving without delay. Thus, the Oakland chapter sold dozens of chapter licenses nationally and internationally to groups of people wanting this idealized lifestyle, and made an enthusiastic, yet unsuccessful foray into Hollywood, leading to a now-cult genre known as "Outlaw Biker" or "Born-to-lose" cinema (the film *Hells Angels 69*, for example, 'starred' many of the people Thompson studied). Interestingly, despite Thompson's warning, his book became a sort of 'how-to' guide for people purchasing chapter licenses (much like Robert Beck's study of Jim-Crow Era prostitution, *Pimp* became popular with street hustlers), the purchasers forgetting, or unaware, the outlaw biker's time Thompson captured had come and gone already. More interesting, however, is the closing of the researcher-research volunteer relationship shared by Thompson and the Hells Angels. Though neither party has stated publically why Thompson was "stomped" (beaten down severely) by the Angels, it can be supposed the motorcycle club, too, forgot Thompson's qualitative research mission. After they allowed themselves to be studied, in the club's attempt to export their identity, which Thompson described always as singular or unique, they saw not enough material benefit (other than license sales and charter dues) to outweigh increased police attention and their placement by general society into larger pop culture, ideologically next to the so-called hippies and other radical social outliers, contrary to what was once a general wish of theirs, to be seen as lone wolves left to themselves.

If people can mistake the opinions of one person or of a few people to be the voice of the many, as can happen while reading qualitative research, an opposite mistake can be imposed during the reading of quantitative research. Here, what casual readers believe they see often during their day-to-day lives may **subvert**, or undermine, what actual data state. In other words, if people may confuse the small for the big in qualitative research, they may also confuse the big for the small in quantitative research; when people ignore what quantitative research has to say, people may think things exist in greater numbers than they do really, or events people observe take place far more frequently than they do actually. Think of it this way: I have mentioned earlier that about 13.5-percent of Americans describe themselves as African-American or black. This is not an especially large percentage, considering the remaining 86.5-percent of Americans do not self-describe as black. However, given the diversity seen easily in today's national-level television programing, where between 33 and 50-percent of talk show and news broadcasts' hosts are black, it would be easy for the casual observer to assume there are far more African-Americans living in The United States than what the Census has accounted for, and particularly easier if the same observer lives in a center of great cultural diversity, like a large city, or a place of instituted diversity, like a college campus, because one may encounter many people from a host of cultural backgrounds daily. Thus, what is taken from casual visual observation can be disproportionate to studied numerical observation. We may then see a possible genesis of the recent Academy Awards' protest—if African-Americans are believed to hold numbers almost three or four times the size of their actual population, as suggested by their participation in televised media, it is little wonder that people became upset when the number of black nominations did not reflect the same level of statistical inflation. As it stands, because African-American film director Spike Lee is to be given an award for a lifetime of direction, when his participation is averaged into the number of all people nominated for an award in direction (five others), it is found, with Lee as a representative, the black community constitutes 16.66-percent of direction-related awards. It would constitute 20-percent if the sample were to remove Alejandro González Iñárritu, a director belonging to the Mexican minority. In either case, a number greater than the 13.5-percent mentioned previously is arrived at, if full demographic representation is to be considered representative of **parity**, or equality, within an Academy Awards' category. Following this thread, for demographic parity to have occurred in awards for best acting ($N=10$), 1.35 members of the black acting community would have to have been nominated, or .675 for either the best male actor ($n^1=5$) or best female actor ($n^2=5$) categories. However, because no black actors of either gender were nominated this year, that the minimum demographic parity was not met (though it is not a factor in the Academy's calculations), let alone the statistically inflated percentages expressed within televised media, a social protest centering around the hashtag "OscarsSoWhite" has formed. In sum, much of the social turmoil we see today seems to have arisen from the general public's confusion surrounding quantitative data. From the Academy Award's controversy, to protests resulting from the common belief more African-Americans die at the hands of law enforcement than Caucasians do as mainstream news media present black deaths more (despite three Caucasians die in violent interactions with police for every one African-American's death), perceived data and actual data are at odds.

Moreover, attention must be given also to an important nuance that is found sometimes in the increasingly more common qualitative-quantitative research method hybrids, where qualitative analyses' typically subjective descriptions may be validated by reimagined statistical data: Once-neutral statistical data can be used as biased rhetorical tools with which to persuade public opinion. For example, consider once more the percentage 13.5, which refers to the size of America's black population today as it relates to the sizes of the nation's other ethnic groups. Again, this is not a comparatively large percentage, and members of the black community have been accorded minority status for that reason (though as the number of African-Americans continues to shrink nationally, the question of whether to assign the group threatened status comes up often). And because America is a representative democracy, where every vote is said to count, this last point takes on an immediate importance; in America, the social body with the most votes is thought to have the most sway politically as it directs national **discourse** or conversation. Thus, academics and political activists, in particular, ask whether it is more **efficacious**, or worthwhile, to cease speaking of an African-American or black population, and refer, instead, in general to *people of color*, a social group which would include African, African-American, Asian, Latin, Middle Eastern, and Native American peoples; doing so, it is imagined, could transform a number of small percentages into one encompassing voting block of about 40-percent of the overall national population. Then again, this idea calls forth also the memory of the Jim Crow-Era 'One Drop Rule,' whereby any non-Caucasian ancestry, at all, rendered an individual non-white, or of color, automatically. Further still, since even the briefest survey of anthropological science tells us no one group is 'pure' racially, that every people to have lived on earth has been subject to ethnic migration and genetic intermingling, the separation of Americans into "white" and "of color" for explicit political benefit is thought, also, by others to walk us back from today's Late Civil Rights Era to something ironically similarly to Apartheid, where the South African government enforced a kind of divide-and-conquer social program through the labeling of people as "white," "colored," and "black". More specifically, complicating our example of cultural **conflation**, or joining is the knowledge those peoples referred to as Europeans today were ancient migrants from Africa, most of today's African-Americans are genetically 24-percent Caucasian, Native Americans migrated from Asia, and the ancestor of all humanity is a black woman.

Premise 7 Review Questions:

To what extent does the use of statistics help you to interpret life's events?

Can math be as descriptive as words? Why? Why not?

How do you feel when others do not share your interpretations of your experiences? Why?

PREMISE 8

Throughout this book, I have questioned how people use research to understand and organize the world—to place an observation in an initial context; to **analyze**, or dissect, the observation; to then **synthesize**, or integrate, meanings belonging to this new observation and previous observations; and to associate comprehension of the observation with the truth. In doing this, I have implied research is a kind of **phenomenology**, or study of events. More so, however, I have suggested research is ultimately an exercise in applied **existentialism**, put generally, the study of being, as I have considered also how public media may choose and distribute selected data gained from a variety of research methods in order to define the world and its peoples in ways that benefit political and social movements often. For the most part, I have spoken of the human both in a general way and in a plural sense, as people. It is now appropriate to consider the individual human as she relates to research. To approach the individual in this singular context, however, a brief summary of the historical **dissemination**, or distribution, of knowledge is necessary.

The study of knowledge is referred to as **epistemology**. Knowledge has not always been the freely traded commodity that it appears to be today; even that most common symbol of free access to reading materials, the public library, is little older than the young United States. Indeed, in the history of the West, at least, it would seem social authorities have given the general public largely unfettered access to the written word only in the last few hundred years, which is quite a small amount of time considering the many thousands of years that humanity has possessed written language forms. That the public library, again, tends to be taken for granted today by a now-literate majority suggests after mere centuries, many people have forgotten advanced learning was considered something sacred, an instrument of God and the State alone during the prior millennia. That the Ancient Greeks thought of *a* library in the Egyptian city of Alexandria to be one of the Seven Wonders of the World, because such a place of learning was exceedingly rare, emphasizes how with a veritable library in each of our IPhones today, collections of printed books are thought often now as redundant. Put simply, few other human endeavors as the comparatively new public knowledge trade have had as much of an impact on the world's democratization, and how severely the leaders of some social institutions in the past reacted to knowledge dissemination by members of the public shows the considerable value this market has held throughout time.

It is no coincidence that one of the first letters to appear in the earliest Western alphabets, the letter 'A,' was written upside down originally; doing so gave the letter the appearance of the head of a domesticated cow, arguably the most valuable commodity in humanity's first permanent settlements—agrarian, or farming, communities. Thus, wealth has been associated with Western written language forms since people struck first upon the idea to record thought. It is also no coincidence writing evolved quickly among the early trade-based Greek and Phoenician city-states, which sought to sell along the Mediterranean seaboard; the ideas of writing and trade empire grew up together as writing facilitated the organization necessary to international commerce greatly. Do not assume, however, writing's initial expansion encouraged mass education programs in the ancient world. On the contrary, formal education was something reserved for the rich almost exclusively. You will recall Homer's poetry belonged to an oral tradition, and was written down only much later; Socrates was illiterate (his student, Plato, transcribed his teachings); and Aristotle, Plato's student, and the person who founded the important school known as the Lyceum, was Alexander the Great's teacher. Nevertheless, because Athens, for instance, was a notably wealthy city, educators to serve this city's many rich sons were in such great demand, that, in addition to Athens encouraging the emigration of foreign scholars from the Italian island of Sicily (known then as a center of technological learning), the city's poorer residents, if they could demonstrate superior analytical skill during the city's popular open debating contests, might hope to rise to the position of tutor, and thus serve the male children of the rich. In this way, Athens' growing number of teachers was a primary reason for the city's reputation as a center of cosmopolitan, or sophisticated, life, and consequently, the city became the chief site from which Rome would import its teaching slaves after the Empire conquered the Greek city-states.

Educational differences within the Ancient Greek and Roman worlds were largely matters of comparative size and intent. In Greece, education was generally the domain of the cultural elite and their servants, but the population of these elite was never immense; yes, the Greek city-states established far-flung trade empires, but one remembers these colonies were really trading posts, and for the most part, the Greeks (not to be confused with their imperialistic northern neighbors, the Macedonians) had little interest in absorbing indigenous cultures surrounding these posts. Rather, with little threat of direct military occupation, peoples trading with the Greeks were left alone to measure the value of Greek culture and language and to choose whether to become Hellenized (culturally Greek). The Roman context was different, however. Given Roman cultural insecurity, insofar anxious Romans had the habit of believing most things Greek, other than warfare, to be superior, the Roman cultural elite tended to purchase Greek teaching slaves to educate their children; the Roman's Latin language would be taught out of a sense of patriotism and because it was the language of the Empire's government and commerce, but the Greek language would be taught, too, out of a desire for so-called sophistication. Next, unlike the Greeks, the Romans had a vested interest in dominating, almost wholly, the indigenous cultures they defeated in battle (religion, though, was by-and-large ignored). The Romans believed making one language, their Latin, the official language of the Empire would sew their racially diverse peoples together: Conquered peoples wanting to appeal to Roman law or to trade with the Romans would have to learn Latin, and to do otherwise would make any group's subjugation utterly complete. Lastly, whereas the Greeks needed only as many merchants who could read and write as their trade demanded, the Romans, who occupied most of the known world, required a near army of literate bureaucrats.

The fascination, if not esteem, many of the public today hold for Ancient Greece and Rome suggests, perhaps, a continuing fondness for a rigidity of social order expressed by cultural and language dominance. Think of how often the phrase, "The Golden Age" is conjured up whenever Greece is called to mind, and how Poe's famous line, "The glory that was Greece and the grandeur that was Rome," is repeated in one's mind whenever one picks up the writing of an ancient author belonging to either culture. It is as if the public today has chosen to ignore Ancient Greece's egotism in favor of its art and Rome's cruelty in favor of its **constancy**, or steadfastness. Because the fruits of the Greek and Roman cultures live on so, we are almost reminded we continue to exist in the shadows of their ruins, and not in our own sunlight, though our own cultures are 1,540-years removed from the ancient world's end (the Western Roman Empire having fallen in 476 AD). And in this way, even as we consider ourselves thoroughly 'modern,' much more of our own moment, we cannot deny the hand of the ancients when we acknowledge Aristotle's discussions of theatre are used to judge the quality of our films, that we build our roads in the Roman way, that our physicians recite the Greek Hippocratic Oath upon entering the practice of medicine, and that Roman law continues to inform North American and European legal codes; the list goes on. Just as we can observe with little effort how the ancient world underpins our lives today 15-centuries after Rome's fall, it is easy to recognize, also, how significantly the ancients lent shape to the lives of earlier people from the aforementioned fall to Europe's Early Modern Period.

In the context of Western education, Christianity has been humanity's worst enemy as well as its best friend. The Church, from The Dark Ages until The Baroque Period, expressed a pivotal anxiety centered upon a perceived catastrophic cultural loss. First, Rome existed as much as an idea as a state. Having existed for almost 1,000-years, Rome had come to represent the eternal, an always (remember, Rome's nickname is "The Eternal City"). In its constancy, Rome had come also to represent an important binary, a border, both literal and figurative, between so-called civilized and uncivilized places and peoples, and though the Romans had persecuted the Christians at first, in becoming Rome's official religion, Christianity was legitimatized and secured for itself all the benefits being Roman in a Roman world had to offer. Problem was, the Empire's western half disintegrated under the weight of migration and internal conflict as The Church was expanding its place in the Roman system. In losing its patron state, The Church was left only with Rome's fascist ideal, which, we will see, it clung to explicitly and implicitly, perhaps as part of what may be described as something akin to an inferiority complex. Second, we understand today that the vast majority of those migrating peoples the Romans had described as barbarians were not the raving hordes of Roman propaganda and today's popular imagination; rather, moving west to avoid devastating raids from nomadic Central Asian tribes, and seeing for themselves the stunning improvements the Romans had made earlier to the Empire's provinces, these peoples, too, imagined a place for themselves somehow within the Empire. This last point fascinates me to no end— foreign peoples, who are said to have tended to esteem Rome more than the Romans, themselves, brought an end to the Rome they respected, less in the sense of having conquered it militarily, but more in the sense of having leaned in on a rotten, hollow core (it says something of the level of Rome's governmental corruption in 476 AD that most historians consider Marcus Aurelius, who reigned about 300-hundred years earlier, from 161-180 AD, to be the last good emperor). Third, The Church found itself thus a symbol of a state, which existed no longer, and the many Northern European tribes to have overwhelmed the state divided the land, which afterward ceased largely to be Roman in name and spirit. Over time, because neither The Church nor the Northern European tribes had wanted to see the stability that Rome had represented once disappear forever, an important series of compromises between them took effect: 1) Understanding to be Roman meant to be civilized, and therefore to be taken seriously, most of the leaders of these pagan tribes, who were now important Western world powers, converted to Christianity because to be late-era Roman was to be Christian. In other words, such was the value of a Roman *ethos* that granting it earned The Church agricultural lands, lands upon which to build churches and monasteries, military protection, the freedom to tax parish inhabitants, the promise to make war upon the pagan tribes to the north and east until they, too, converted to Christianity, and the understanding that Roman law will be used exclusively in cases involving peoples inhabiting the Empire prior to its fall (tribal laws would be applied to tribal affairs). 2) The new aristocracy would not dominate The Church, but would coexist with it, in a manner of twin governments: the former would govern affairs of state (often with Church input and consent), and the latter would govern affairs of the soul as well as educate royalty and provide them with priests educated in law and trained in bureaucracy. 3) Most important to our study, the Roman language, Latin, would continue to be the language of The Church. Latin was also to be the one tongue for those institutions The Church was now responsible for, such as education (and thus, science) and the law (as it pertained to former Roman citizens), as well as the social gears it would influence, like politics (Latin served as a **lingua franca**, or a way to communicate agreed-upon by speakers of different languages, until shifts in world power made French the common political tongue roughly a millennium later, followed by English around the start of the twentieth century).

Though The Church forbade its officers the use of physical violence, a right granted to secular rulers, it carried on nevertheless Imperial Rome's essential fascist spirit of singularity. The Empire's implied central thesis—one emperor, one state, one voice—was revised by The Church, after 476 AD, to be one pope, one Christendom (Christian land), one voice. The Church, likewise, organized its priesthood in a way similar to the Roman Army's basic units, the *centuriae*, headed by *centuriones*, with bishops heading groups of priests, and abbots heading groups of monks. Thus, The Church set itself up as an enduring social institution throughout Europe that resembled the dictatorship Rome had become, yet its sustenance came not from applied violence, as the Empire had depended on, but from control of ideas founded upon the threat of violence (people having been found guilty of breaking Church law would be given over to secular authorities for physical punishments). In a word, The Church saw its power resting in its control of the means of knowledge production.

Today, with so many information streams available to us so immediately, it is perhaps difficult to imagine only one source of information existing, and it is maybe as equally difficult to imagine being without the ability to read. However, this was the reality for most of Europe prior to The Protestant Reformation. As in the Roman world, education could be had if one was wealthy, or if one showed exceptional intellectual promise, but in the post-Empire context, and in both royal and landed homes especially, education was essential for second-born sons because, in the main, only first-born sons inherited property; a second son had generally two choices if he was to survive in the world outside of his childhood home, enter the priesthood or become a soldier. Therefore, the wealthy and land-owning families became more-and-more tied socially to The Church, and it is little coincidence that through time The Church became as socially conservative as the aristocracy (remember, during the French Revolution's Reign of Terror, royal and priest were equal targets). Even so, most ordinary Western Europeans of the time were illiterate and poor, these being social conditions favorable to The Church and its expansion, considering the powers each priest with a parish held. For example, though most priests were fluent in Latin and the languages of their parishioners, Mass was to be held in Latin only. It did not matter if most of a church's parishioners could not understand the Latin of their prayers as that was beside the point; it was enough that the parishioners were in the presence of the language of authority, and mouthed the language without comprehending it completely (interestingly, the Latin Mass continued until 1964). Further still, the Bible and other religious texts were to be written in Latin only, as well, because The Church put forth a priest was to be a community's singular translator of the divine word into the **vernacular**, or local language, believing the common people generally too ignorant to convey this knowledge articulately, meaningfully, or responsibly. Hence, The Church, as an institution, in selecting for itself a language mostly non-native to a Europe reshaped culturally after Rome's fall, in keeping to an education schema more than a few millennia old (despite assisting in the creation of a new institution, the university), and in positioning priests as gatekeepers to knowledge, effectively controlled learning for almost 1,000 years, until around 1490, when the newly invented printing press offered something largely unknown to The Church—competition.

The printing press troubled The Church greatly because, as with the earlier Roman power structure, it could not tolerate the suggestion of an alternative to itself; the merest possibility of opposition was as fearful a prospect as open rebellion. Which is to say, public access to this new technology represented an existential threat to The Church on many fronts: 1) Western Europeans now had unimagined access to educational materials, like books, which needed not to be written in Latin and interpreted by priests, but in their own languages, and they could now assemble their own personal libraries, having no longer to enter into the monastic life if one wished to live surrounded by books. 2) Western Europeans, being very religious in those days, hoped for themselves copies of the Bible translated into their own languages so they could become closer to their faith, though The Church saw fulfillment of this desire to be encouraging an unheard-of level of personal **agency**, or empowerment, that would only devalue the social power of its agents, the priests, considerably—a gatekeeper, after all, needs a gate to watch over; he is otherwise redundant. 3) For The Church, translation meant much more than merely rewriting one language into another. The Church believed translation to be an open door to both reinterpretation of its official Bible, the *Versio Vulgata* (known commonly today as the Vulgate), and interpretation of newly found scriptures coming from the East. 4) In Western Europe, with the Frankish Empire standing behind the early Popes, Latin remained the language of The Church unquestioningly. However, in Eastern Europe, the Franks' rival, the Byzantine Empire, contrary to Church doctrine, allowed its citizens to worship in the Greek language, and more-or-less allowed the peoples neighboring it to worship in their native tongues, the result of which was the growth of several churches, and each with its own patriarch, or male leader (that the leaders of the Catholic and Russian Orthodox Churches just met officially in 2016, almost 1,000-years after East broke from West in The Great Schism, suggests the sting The Church felt). 5) The Church saw itself as a *logos*-based institution, concerned more with the law of God, whilst the churches to have formed in the East, with their greater interest in God's mystery, were based on *pathos*. The Church was thus concerned that unauthorized, impassioning interpretations of the Bible could only decentralize orderly Western European religious life, especially if these interpretations were represented in a plurality of languages. Yet, as to this last point, history shows us The Church was never quite fond of overt religious enthusiasm, anyway, even before the printing press appeared. Recall it was common for The Church to have more radical and passionate religious groups within its sphere of influence executed for heresy (think of the Cathars in southern France), or to maintain social control during periods of mass hysteria (as happened to the Flagellants during The Black Death and other calamities). Nevertheless, history shows us also that The Church was correct in its fears of the new printing technology, as cynical as those fears may have been.

Put simply, The Protestant Reformation is the reason most of us are educated today. The movement's **crux**, or root, was found in the revolutionary belief that people are to attain, through formal education, the reading ability and critical thinking skills necessary to allow them to read, in their own languages, the Bible with the specific intention of finding personal meaningfulness in it for themselves. To give a man the ability to read was believed to encourage a closer, more immediate, relationship between him and God because he, and not a priest-interpreter, will have wrestled for himself his own substantial understandings of God and God's relationship with humanity; a man who is educated has been freed from a life of anonymous purposelessness within the historical cathedral's congregation. Moreover, a person better able to articulate his own understandings of the Bible, it was thought, was better able to motivate others to seek their own understandings after hearing his public evangelization, or preaching of the Christian Gospel. In this way, The Protestant Reformation moved to form a public **dialectic**, or discussion of the truth within interpretations, whereas The Roman Church seemed to remain content with its memorized catechistic, or call and response, program.

Now, though this crux was central to the eventual democratization of education (as it held all Christians, and not just a cultural elite (priests, for instance), are capable of attaining intellectual and spiritual maturities), the political motivation behind The Protestant Reformation was seldom wholly democratic in intent. Yes, religious agitation against The Church took root in Northern Europe, and yes, the growing middle class' desire for education there coincided with The Reformation's call to education, but it was the German princes (and later, the English royalty), who saw a material advantage to this symbiosis set up upon education. Northern German states and the England of Henry VIII grew increasingly disturbed by having to coexist with a twin government, whose head, the Pope, was far way in Rome, and after about 1,400-years, sought no longer input and consent in political matters from what was considered thereon as The Roman Church. Before the rise of the printing press, The Roman Church held royalty in check with the implied threat of excommunication, or spiritual expulsion from the Christian community; after excommunication, a Christian state's citizens would be forbidden by The Church to follow the now-heathen leader, and The Church would be free then to suggest the degraded individual's more cooperative replacement. However, the Northern European royalty understood full well if they were to promote the newly formed, and socially popular, Protestant Churches, and most importantly back them militarily, they would not have to fear excommunication because their peoples would have to be behind them, or face the abrupt, grim reality of being sent to the burning stake by The Roman Church for heresy, or dissent. Thus, for the high price of The Thirty Years' War fought against The Roman Church and its allies (with the War's approximately 7.5 million people dead), the leaders of Northern Europe gained independence from The Roman Church's sphere of political and social influence, the Protestant Churches thrived, and education began to take the form we recognize.

The university or college we know today is seen best as a set of bridges linking us to the Scotland and Germany of the Early Modern Age, The Age of Enlightenment, and especially The Romantic Age, which followed both eras, and is when the basic idea of higher education bloomed full flower. We have the Scots, for instance, to thank for reimagining and establishing higher education's core class program (in the Scottish context, English, Greek, history, Latin, math, philosophy, religion, and science classes), and the Germans to thank for what we take now to be a given, the idea of majoring in a favorite subject, as opposed to merely checking-off a list of core classes determined by one's year in school. In a way, a student at university today, whether she knows it or not, is reenacting The Protestant Reformation each semester. Most likely a commoner, this individual is employing her ability to read to interpret for herself her assigned readings, to decide for herself the truth of her assigned readings, and to choose for herself which ideas from her assigned readings to incorporate into her personal and professional lives. And just as the education-positive tone of Scotland and Germany led, in part, to both nations becoming scientific powerhouses later during The Industrial Revolution, the student's level of intellectual maturity is, today, limited chiefly by her desire to learn now that she has the freedom to learn—so important is education considered today, that most people equate it as a basic human right. Yet, it would be incorrect to think The Protestant Reformation's effects on education were felt immediately by all members of society; recall the eyes of people enslaved in the Pre-Civil War United States could be removed if they were caught reading, higher education was thought generally to be wasted on women, as I have mentioned earlier, until about 1900, and the male working poor, though encouraged to learn enough to be functionally literate, were discouraged from learning too much, lest they forget their station, or social position, in life and agitate for better working conditions more eloquently. And when I look at my students, I realize most of them are, as was I, only in a university or college classroom because public financial aid has existed, beyond the GI Bill and traditional scholarships, for about the last four-and-a-half decades.

One may feel demoralized, knowing until the last half-century higher education was for the most part, to put it charitably, a boys' club; it was during The Industrial Revolution, when males from the ever-larger middle class, in appreciable numbers, began to move past grade school and join their wealthy counterparts at university or college. The female presence in higher education rose later; the rise in female representation corresponding generally to their gaining of the right to vote—in the 1920's. Members of ethnic minorities joined higher education more representatively several decades later, mostly after the end of the segregationist Jim Crow Laws. Despite the glacial pace of inclusion within higher education, and of the greatest importance to our study, The Protestant Reformation's central idea, personal ownership of idea, wilted only under the severest of fascist regimes, like those of the Nazis and Imperial Japanese; even in racist Jim Crow America, the subjugation of African-Americans was never so complete as to extinguish the idea of a better future for themselves totally. That said, what exactly does our freedom to own an idea mean?

Consider Galileo, a scientist, who lived during the time of the initial **wane**, or decline, of the Roman Church's considerable political and social powers. One suspects an idea of his, that the earth rotates around the sun, and not *vice versa*, landed him in real trouble with The Inquisition not because what he put forth was untrue (The Church admitted his idea was a possibility), but because, rather, he stuck to his idea in the face of explicit Church opposition to it. In context, what a person learned during pre-Protestant Reformation higher education was meant to be used to elevate God's, and by extension, The Church's, glory and authority; The Renaissance was much of an exercise in faith as it was an energetic reclamation of Ancient Greek and Roman sciences and technologies. Therefore, although Galileo would have likely imagined his idea as beneficial to humanity because it increased humanity's body of knowledge,
The Church, regardless of the idea's merit, saw the idea's very presentation as a rude affront: The Church's agents had little use for Galileo's work because they did not come up with the idea, themselves, nor had they condoned it with the intention of incorporating the idea into accepted science. Today, on the other hand, it is notably difficult to think of individual and idea as separate from one another when considering higher education (though, this year, Larycia Hawkins was forced out of her professorship at Wheaton College, a Christian school, for her idea of Christian and

Muslim unity, which she expressed by wearing a *hijab*, or headscarf, for a day). From a student's first day at university or college, she learns her grades in classes centered on critical thinking will be dependent largely on the originality and thoroughness of her idea; only the most basic of courses are centered on rote memorization, anymore. Truly, as a writing professor, I can hardly imagine pressing my students to repeat a philosophical or political line as, to me, doing so would be unethical; I have been encultured long in the idea of encouraging, but not shaping, student thought. And I would go so far as saying my chief struggle, as a writing professor, is to ensure my students are not parroting my ideas because: 1) to mimic is too easy (growth is one result of struggle); 2) if the institutionalism within grade school is based on a remnant fascist urge, compelling my students to think for themselves may embolden them to leave their institutionalization behind (one should note the sheer terror on some of my students' faces when I tell them calling me "Doctor" is optional in my classroom); and 3) the average citizen is called upon to be a follower, and not a leader, in society enough (my students do not need to ape me, too). Indeed, I find it especially useful to employ a different, ever-more challenging subject theme each semester; a comfortable, worn-out topic runs the risk of promoting intellectual laziness in me and my students.

It all comes down to ***ethos***. Recall *ethos* is an Ancient Greek term referring to a person's **character**, or moral strength, the level of **credibility**, or trustworthiness, a person is thought by her peers to possess, and also a person's reputation within her community; of special significance to us is the knowledge that a person's *ethos* is thought, moreover, to be a publically-assigned quality, concurrently born with (as in basic human rights, but also as in stereotypes surrounding an individual from birth) and earned over a lifetime (as in ranking within society), but lost surprisingly easily after an unfortunate moment or an unpleasant social interaction. A person's level of *ethos*, at least on paper, then, is something the individual has been granted, for better or worse, and is not something the individual can claim for herself without appearing self-congratulating (a notable public exception to this last point being the freedom to brag given the emcee role in historically African-American rap music as the audacity is seen as **emancipatory**, or socially-freeing). It goes without saying most of us wish for a high *ethos*, and as I have suggested earlier, the question of ethos has been the underlying basis for most of the Civil Rights movements during this and the previous centuries. Note, too, how our conception of *ethos* has been tied historically to *logos* (again, meaning the word, text, or logic) as *logos* is related to idea. For example, at first, in the Ancient Greek world, *ethos* was determined by a man's ability to communicate an idea persuasively; in the Ancient Roman world, by his ability to serve The State unquestioningly; in the Medieval world guided by The Church, by his ability to be docile and to **transcend**, or rise above, inherent human flaws expressed by Original Sin, or the so-called characteristically human predisposition to behave wrongly; in the Protestant Reformation world, by his ability to promote trade and to live, nevertheless, in a godly way; in The Age of Enlightenment world, by his ability to live logically; in The Romantic Age (known also as The Age of Revolution), by his *or her* ability to live passionately; and in The Industrial Revolution world, by his ability to accumulate wealth and to contribute materially to ever-expanding scientific and technological progresses. To describe *ethos* within Twentieth and Twenty-First Century contexts is, however, a much more difficult task because our time has seen so many diametrically opposed ideas gain such wide social popularity contemporaneously; recent history has shown it is just as easy for a person to gain the public esteem of *ethos* for promoting imperialist, racist, and sexist points-of-view as it is for promoting anti-colonialism, tolerance, and humanism. We exist in a time of *zeitgeists*, and not *zeitgeist*.

We are living also at the beginning of the Post-Postmodernist Age. Perhaps the social discord surrounding media today is one result of an **ideological**, or conceptual, shift from the cynical and permissive postmodernism I have discussed earlier in this book to a more rationalist mindset; a movement from a rigorously socially-policed (as in politically correct) acknowledgement of multiple, if not endless, lived subjectivities to the use of a more objective, and less socially divisive, **lens**, or worldview. Consider an especially popular, *ethos*-centered verbal defense: "You don't know me. You can't judge me". In the postmodern context, this defense makes perfect sense—it suggests the speaker's and listener's subjective realities are different enough materially that the listener does not possess the privilege to understand the speaker or her behaviors, history, and intentions; that the speaker's *ethos* remains intact, unquestionable, even, because whatever judgment may be behind a possible description of her moral strength, trustworthiness, or reputation is **moot**, or highly debatable, from the start. However, today, there seems also to be a concurrent preference for more nuanced analyses based on another important, and reclaimed, Ancient Greek belief, that public acts and speech belong no longer to the doer or speaker once performed or spoken. The Socratic school, for instance, held actions and words are so powerful simply because they involve an immediate transference of social power from *rhetor* to audience; public **scrutiny**, or examination, will follow most any social interaction. That said, the Ancient Greeks thought one's participation in social discourse is invariably a dangerous activity because one's deeds and words will see one either glorified, ignored, or **rebuked** (criticized) publically. And thus, while the person to have declared, "You don't know me. You can't judge me" meant, in essence, "I exist outside of your scrutiny, and I am left, then, to glory in my own sense of self," her public may now remind her one cannot have it 'both ways'; one cannot commit to an action or express an opinion in the public sphere without the expectation of being responded to by the public; to expect so would be naïve, or socially immature. Our psychiatric community offers us an interesting third approach: Center response upon the quality of the person's actions and words, but not upon the quality of the person, herself. However, this rhetorical position has, outside of a medical or therapeutic context, the effect of separating action from actor and message from messenger. In sum, today, a person may not expect to have her communication responded to, in keeping with that fading postmodernist value (and she may call forth assertions of racism, sexism, and/or white guilt and privilege in an era-approved strategy to defend and maintain self-sovereignty of *ethos*), or she may expect to have her communication responded to, in keeping with the post-postmodernist reminder that social discourse is an ongoing conversation (and see changes in her level of *ethos* as indicative of her success or failure at persuading others), or she may expect to have her communication responded to specifically in the context of a public reaction to her response to what has interested her, and not in the context of the person who she is, in keeping with the aforementioned reconciliation implied by work done in the psychiatric community (and see *ethos* granted to or removed from her idea, but not her). Communication is messy when one era is ending and another is beginning. It is not as if light switches are turned off and on; rather, long-held ideas will coexist with new ideas for quite some time until the newer era overshadows the older almost completely.

Reconsider an article of clothing I have mentioned earlier, the popular T-shirt saying "Unapologetically Black", and think of the many social responses that the wearing of it may or may not inspire among the public. For example, to wear it publically in the postmodern sense is to suggest no response is desired by the wearer; it is enough to observe one has chosen to purchase and wear it for one's own reasons. Asking the wearer about this clothing choice in this context may evoke a defensive response, particularly since the stated message's first word, "unapologetically" suggests explicitly the conversation has ended before it has begun. Whether or not the wearer and observer agree upon a definition of blackness, beyond the most basic physical state of one having melaninated skin, is irrelevant. For the wearer, her *ethos* the day she wears the T-shirt is set in the declaration that she is her own definition of "black"; she is independent of the observer's definition, and worries little about measuring up to other peoples' definitions, anyway. It is here we begin to understand why a majority of postmodern writings are centered on the existence of difference, and descriptions of difference, and, yet, not so much upon critiques of difference beyond investigations of the historical evils of cultural- and state-enforced social discrimination. Put simply, works exploring an alternative to difference—the shared humanity of peoples, or a oneness of humanity, are few-and-far-between in the postmodern library because as I have put forth earlier, since World War Two, postmodernism has regarded research of human **homogeneity**, or similarity, as politically and culturally suspicious, and the scholar pursuing such work as terribly naïve, at best, or as a person with a fascist bent, at worst. Within postmodernism's **orthodoxy**, or accepted beliefs, even the idea that difference is not total may be considered a racist idea for exactly whom does it benefit to see cultural difference **effaced**, or erased? One train of postmodernist thought suggests, for instance, cultural assimilation profits only the cultural majority as members of cultural minorities are to assume the goals and values of the majority whilst discarding their own. And another train of postmodernist thought suggests, almost contradictorily to the last point, a cultural majority is dependent upon the existence of minority groups in order to maintain what society knows to be artificial binaries, as in, for example, 'your blackness confirms my whiteness.' Thus, postmodernist research has been seen recently as a limited, almost one-person conversation, and it is not surprising that in a postmodern word, Ta-Nehisi Coates is **lauded**, or praised, for suggesting the lived experience of the American black male is a unique one, and Stacey Dash is demonized for suggesting unquestioned belief in the self-described uniqueness of social groups renders the national body weaker. Comedian Chris Rock implied the **saliency**, or importance, of Dash's demonization when he had her appear before the recent Academy Awards to wish the audience a happy Black History Month, which she is opposed to as a negative expression of self-segregation. Postmodernism, in its furtherance of cultural diversity, like the extreme political left, appears to be uncomfortable with intellectual diversity.

To wear the aforementioned T-shirt in the post-postmodern sense, however, is to suggest a social response is desired by the wearer; the purchasing and wearing of a provocative garment are choices made by the individual with the intention of provoking conversation. Asking the wearer about this clothing choice in this latter context will, most likely, arouse a positive response, despite the stated message's strong tone; here, "unapologetically" is meant more in the sense of 'Ask me why I am unapologetic", and less in the sense of "Do not bother asking me; you simply would not understand", as suggested by the older postmodern context. Whether or not the wearer and observer can agree upon a definition of blackness takes on, perhaps, the greatest importance because definition and **consensus**, or agreement, are ideas to be investigated **bilaterally** (jointly), and especially in a civil manner. Both wearer and observer resist seeing the production of knowledge as **unilateral** (one-sided) or as a necessary social competition, and for the wearer, her *ethos* is set by how logical her observer takes her point-of-view to be. Moreover, the wearer understands her idea is not independent of the observer's definition because she is interested in how her idea measures up to other peoples' definitions. Given post-postmodernism's comparative youth, we see its ideals expressed most often today within the comment sections of social media postings. For example, a year ago one would have been hard pressed to find counterarguments following the many race-based articles National Public Radio (NPR) posted on its *Facebook* newsfeed. Indeed, so uncommon was a divergence of thought from NPR's postmodernist underpinnings that the rare individual to offer **dissent**, or disagreement, online tended to be **excoriated**, or criticized fully, by devoted page followers rather quickly. Today, though, so common are readers' calls for more objectivity within NPR's reporting of race relations that these comments more-often-than-not appear before wholly favorable reader responses, unquestioning fans wonder aloud now what has become of NPR's comments section (NPR being a traditional home to orthodox social liberalism), and most strikingly, posted threats to contact a dissenter's employer with the intention of having him or her fired for his or her viewpoints appear now to have dwindled substantially. In a word, post-postmodernism is comfortable with intellectual diversity (as in new ideas promote new conversations, and not in the sense of a policed diversity-for-diversity's sake), and unlike postmodernism, it considers intellectual health to be a matter of **cognitive receptivity**, or intellectual openness, beyond a continuous public acknowledgement of almost-irreconcilable social differences.

To wear the "Unapologetically Black" T-shirt in the third way (with its therapeutic basis, and its existence outside of the postmodern and post-postmodern senses), argues a social response to the article of clothing, itself, is desired by the wearer; the choices to purchase and to wear the T-shirt are observed as existing in a context specific to place and time, and with having **catharsis**, or emotional and intellectual releases, in mind. Asking the wearer about her clothing choice in this framework may inspire the wearer to **delineate**, or outline, the feeling and logic behind her wearing of it that day for the observer. The observer, then, imparts an initial sense of agency, or social power, to the wearer; *ethos* is extended, like credit, by the observer until that time the wearer proves the quality of her thinking to be less than trustworthy. Most importantly, because the observer's inquiry is limited to the wearing, and does not stretch to the wearer, the wearer becomes free to alter her *stasis* (initial position), *thesis* (argument), and choice of evidences to communicate more effectively in the future, should she wear the T-shirt again. The observer does not characterize the wearer for who she is, but rather by what she says, and how she revises what she says. Given the gentleness and patience of this approach, the give-and-take of this third manner of communication is seen seldom in public discourse.

It is easy to think of *ethos* as an especially **fickle**, or changeable, quality, particularly when one knows how easily it may be lost by an individual, even after a lifetime of hard work. In the Ancient Greek sense of it, *ethos* is perhaps the most affecting reflection of the public's mood toward the individual, fairly or unfairly, and here one is reminded immediately of the old idea, that which gives can take away. Moreover, it is interesting how often, in our world today, we are told by our friends and families to just be ourselves, and to not to give what others may think of us a second thought (which one probably senses now is, in itself, a postmodern idea). Even so, that individual with a strong, learned sense of self will likely come to realize both she and her ideas will be judged publicly throughout her life as she will mix socially with the public. Crocodiles have thick armor for a reason— other crocodiles. Like it or not, most of us will have to work for a living, which means being appreciated enough by others to pass occasional work performance reviews, and we will have to move about on the street and interact otherwise with our neighbors, which means conforming at least to the most basic of socially-acceptable behaviors. Those more private people who choose to work from home and order their groceries and clothes on the Web are not exempt from the public's gaze, either, as businesses are known to mine data almost ceaselessly from personal electronic interactions to define, and then guide, the people's browsing and purchasing behaviors. Likewise, even the most introverted people probably maintain active, albeit more anonymous, social lives on the Internet, which means they, too, conform to normative social values ('norms'), in this case, the rules of their various Web communities, lest they be seen, and then excluded socially, as 'trolls', or meddling troublemakers. And almost all people on the Web will wear ***personae***, or masks, metaphorically in order to present themselves in the best, most *ethical* light as mingling in social media is a performance, considering the labor involved in the choosing, editing, and filtering that go into that most basic visual presentation of ourselves, the avatar (my students tell me it takes, on average, about an hour or two to arrange an acceptable *Facebook* profile picture, which may then be changed throughout the day). The point is the Ancient Greeks understood people to be social creatures existing in a world of social cause-and-effect. The Romans, as evidenced by Ovid's *Metamorphoses* and Marcus Aurelius' *Meditations*, thought one constant in people's lives is change; as all things are subject to mutation, the fame, for example, a person holds one day may be turned into infamy the next, only to have this infamy mutate back to fame later on because social contexts change often, too. Millennia later, Freud reminded us much of society's despair is based upon this essential **tension**, or stress: most humans find more material benefit in joining together as communities than in living alone; however, one can never truly be oneself in a community. Because most communities will enforce rules (manners and laws, for instance) to maintain all-important social **cohesion**, or unity, the individual will be called upon to hold back on expressing herself fully or face social or legal punishment; to exist outside of the social norm is to be without *ethos*, and to be considered a social deviant, or misfit, until she conducts herself again publically in ways reflecting the values of her community. Further still, Maslow tells us social affection is as important to human life as is food and shelter, and similarly, Buscaglia theorizes the nausea felt after an argument with a respected peer or during a break-up with a romantic partner is, perhaps, a vestigial response to the paralyzing fear of being deserted that prehistoric humans held; being excluded socially, after all, meant certain death at the hands of rival clans, as prey to wild animals, or as a result of exposure to hunger and the elements. *Ethos* is linked, thus, to survival.

We have seen the high importance people give to *ethos*, and we recognize the granting of it as a possible cause of anxiety within the public. So important is acknowledgement from others, Freud suggests, that the individual, under the debilitating influence of social stress, grants equal weight to positive and negative attentions illogically; the important thing is the person is being paid attention to—she matters to others presently, and is not being ignored, despite any later, behavior-based social ramifications. In this way, today, we tend also to give fame and infamy equal weight. To say we confuse infamy for fame would not be quite precise as though the natures of infamy and fame are defined by people as being much different, their effect on public conversation is largely the same in the short term. Think of a person to have become a household name, Kim Kardashian. Her celebrity rose out of infamy; in her case, a scandal involving a leaked sex tape. In a word, she transformed her appearance in what can be considered a pornographic film into a media presence worth more than sixty million dollars. That she is ever-present in media today suggests she is important to the public, but whether she is actually taken seriously by the public is open to question. Is Kardashian's current fame based upon traits associated historically with *ethos*—her character (moral strength), or the level of credibility (trustworthiness) the public thinks her to possess, or her good reputation in society? Fame is thought by most to be also the result of rare talent or noted heroism, but infamy to be the result of inability, cowardice, moral weakness, dishonesty, or disrepute. Perhaps time decides the lastingness of public acknowledgement. Will, for example, Kardashian be remembered in 100-years, or will she be forgotten once the public becomes bored with her televised antics?

Then again, when we consider the lack of intellectual **rigor**, or attention, the public seems now to apply when assigning fame or infamy to an individual, we understand the idea of *ethos* may have become a bit muddled. As one who studies language for a living, few other terms make me cringe as much as the currently popular and rhetorically weak, 'slut-shaming'. This term, meaning to criticize one socially for one's suspected promiscuous behavior, is used actually in defense of the criticized individual, as in, 'Stop shaming the slut'. Therein is the problem. On the one hand, the people to call slut-shaming out are assigning *ethos* to the individual in question, inasmuch no human is to be shamed for engaging in human behaviors; however, the same people are suggesting the individual who may engaged in a consensual, adult relationship is, in fact, a 'slut', a term that points toward infamy strongly outside of Third-Wave Feminist and postmodern communities, who have attempted to reclaim the word as a positive. Given it is safe to assume most other people have not transformed 'slut' into a positive noun, it is enough for concerned people to tell community members prying into the life of the individual, instead, to 'Mind your own business'; doing so assigns the attacked individual *ethos* without calling her dignity into question.

This is a simple idea, and I am surprised the term is as socially popular as it is.

A summary of our discussion of *ethos* is found easily in an analysis of Beyoncé Knowles' *Super Bowl 50* halftime performance, during which the singer performed the comparatively less-political, first-half of her song, "Formation". As a whole, the song addresses three topics common to public discourse today: black pride, government inaction in historically black communities (as in its delayed response to the devastation brought on by Hurricane Katrina), and violent interactions between some police officers and members of the black community. The performance, itself, presented three **analogous**, or similar, visual themes: the close-fisted Black Power salute, costumes suggestive of uniforms worn by The Black Panther Party, and an "X" dancer formation, which brought to mind slain Civil Rights leader, Malcolm X. Though new, the song was not unknown to the public, its video having been released in the days leading up to *The Super Bowl*. And Knowles, a super-star, was certainly known already by most of the audience.

Prior to the halftime show, Knowles enjoyed a generally comfortable *ethos*; any infamy assigned to the singer was centered on her modeling work for L'Oréal Cosmetics, which appeared to have lightened her skin in advertisements year-by-year after she left the band, Destiny's Child. Nevertheless, this criticism gained little traction among the public because the choices to wear pale makeup and blonde hair tend to be seen, and defended, as personal decisions (despite increasingly-strident counterarguments put forth by the ever-more popular Team Dark Skin and Team Natural (hair) movements), and, anyway, Knowles had donated significant bail monies for people arrested during Black Lives Matter-led protests. Thus, just prior to the showcasing of her new song, Knowles was at the height of her social power, accepted largely as a socially "safe", or non-offensive, easily marketable, commodity by most American communities.

Reconfiguring of the singer's *ethos* started shortly after the "Formation" video was released, with the most public attention and scrutiny given to the phrase, "Stop shooting us" spray-painted on one of the set's walls. Murmurings among the law-and-order crowd, whom I referred to earlier as The Silent Majority, described Knowles as anti-police, lowering her *ethos* within socially-conservative communities thusly. However, that a super-star, like Knowles, had so much to lose materially by speaking to such a heated social issue so explicitly, and because she was thought to be speaking honestly by more social activism-minded people, her *ethos* rose within socially-liberal communities thusly. The general public was left to wonder, then, what her *Super Bowl 50* halftime performance would have to offer. Her performance's visual themes would prove to be strong, but would be found to be based upon historical abstractions, as well: the close-fisted Black Power salute called to mind the Civil Rights Movement, especially as it was used in protest at the 1968 Olympics, but it was used also to punctuate Knowles' embracing of her black identity; the back-up dancers' costumes suggested the uniforms worn by the racial separatist Black Panther Party, at least from the waist-up (short-shorts were definitely not standard issue Black Panther uniform), and reminded the public of the racial divisiveness of the later Civil Rights Movement, especially after Martin Luther King, Jr.'s assassination; and the "X" dancer formation, which brought to mind assassinated Civil Rights leader, Malcolm X, brought to mind X's less-pacifist, more-direct action philosophy, too. Put simply, Knowles' presentation was provocative enough socially to see her *ethos* fall and rise concurrently. Possibly more injurious to her *ethos* in the immediate future will be her choice of concert security. In Miami, Florida, a representative of a police union called for officers to refuse providing security for Knowles'

concerts, after which Louis Farrakhan, leader of The Nation of Islam, offered his followers as security. Given Farrakhan confessed on *60 Minutes* to being complicit in the murder of Malcolm X, the leader whom Knowles **lauded**, or praised, in her halftime show, one wonders
if people, black activists especially, will see Knowles' acceptance of Farrakhan's offer as hypocritical, and thus as infamous. Is it ethical to hire one who had a hand in the murder of a Civil Rights hero?

Premise 8 Review Questions:

What is the level of your ethos?

What criteria do you use when assigning ethos to another person?

Should the concept of ethos be done away with?

CODA

My inspiration for this book was found in the title of a collection of Raymond Carver's short stories, *What people talk about when they talk about love*. I had just completed a long day of grading student research papers. My thoughts were centered equally on exhaustion (I write a whole heck of a lot of notes on the essays I read), jealousy (I grade about 150-papers each grading cycle, so there is simply no time for my own writing for weeks at a time), and imagination (I take true delight in following each of the many intellectual paths my students take in their writing), and in my favorite way of unwinding after work, I was browsing in a thrift store when I spotted Carver's book. His title got me to thinking about research, as my mind had not yet separated itself fully from the day's grading. In my mind, I transformed Carver's title, *What people talk about when they talk about love* to *What people think about when they think about research.* I felt I was on to something, perhaps because the more papers I graded, the more I longed for my own research project, but likely more so because whenever I grade, I feel keenly protective of my students. I have taught writing since 1998, and with each new semester, my nagging suspicion that the information available to students is of an increasingly lesser quality grows further. In a word, the vast quantity of research materials available to students today does not necessarily mean sincere quality of research materials available to students today. It was in Amvets' musty aisles that I decided to begin a text, after my grading was completed, which would encourage beginning writers to question the value, and the rhetorical intent behind, those materials that students will find when performing their assigned research.

I am different from my students insofar the first half of my life was lived before the transformative rise of computer technology. My **formative**, or foundational, years saw me leading my own search for reading materials, my choosing of specific texts, out of very many on the same subject, on my own, and my learning to judge, according to my own developing values, the intellectual quality of whatever media struck my interest. Therefore, I was never sold on the idea of the 'Information Superhighway' said to be provided by the Internet. As if a Steve Jobs or a Bill Gates would not tell us the technology they are peddling is all that, and a bag of chips. Because I had learned to depend on myself, and my own efforts brought me to graduate school, I viewed the rise of computer technology with the suspicion of a primary-level math teacher who finds her student using a calculator. Maybe most **galling**, or annoying, to me was education,
itself, seemed to be so completely spellbound with the idea of computers in the classroom; to me,
the general scholastic call to turn hard-earned, yet exceedingly profitable, personal relationships with books into

a few mere key strokes struck into a search box seemed just plain laziness on the part of my colleagues. Most student will do as they are told, and will believe what they are taught, so if they are told the computer is the best way to research by their teachers, they are left to believe the quality of whatever materials the Internet offers them has to be good. My suspicion, nevertheless, bore out a few years into the rise of computers when we learned search engines have the nasty habit of accepting money from information clearinghouses to place their materials first; I am the type of professor to feel badly when a commercial sneaks itself into a video clip I show to a class—the minds of students are to be influenced only by academic, and not commercial, information. More devastating to student intellectual development, though, is the synthesis, or combination, of this encouraged lack of academic rigor with the common student belief today that all voices are to be given equal weight, that humans are not to be judged. We laugh at the joke, "It's on the Internet, so it must be true", but many people, students especially, hold this premise to be Gospel fact.

Further, I enjoy my work as a teacher and researcher, but I find myself disappointed largely by the common lack of thorough analyses with which data belonging to today's scholarship are presented in media; more often than not, it seems we are asked now to 'accept each other's stories' rather than to interrogate truth objectively—and rigorously. The information one takes to be true is thought often, also, to be declared allegiance to one school of thought or another, and the distribution of information tends, now, to take on an air of pandering to true believers. I dare say I miss the days when even the smallest news item presented two points of view.

Works Consulted

Aurelius, Marcus. *Meditations*. Mineola, NY: Dover Publications, 1997. Print.

"Authors Of 'All American Boys' Talk About How Book Has Sparked Race Discussion." *NPR*. NPR, 5 Jan. 2016. Web. 11 Mar. 2016.

Baker, Kelly J. "Dear Liberal Professor, Students Aren't The Problem." *Vitae, the Online Career Hub for Higher Ed*. The Chronicle of Higher Education, 10 June 2015. Web. 12 Mar. 2016.

Baumeister, Roy F. *Evil: Inside Human Violence and Cruelty*. New York: Henry Holt, 2001. Print.

Black, Thomas R. *Doing Quantitative Research in the Social Sciences: An Integrated Approach to Research Design, Measurement and Statistics*. London: Sage Publications, 1999. Print.

Buscaglia, Leo F. *Love*. Greenwich, CT: Fawcett, 1972. Print.

Carver, Raymond. *What We Talk about When We Talk about Love*. London: Harvill, 1998. Print.

Chapple, Christopher R., and William D. Steers. *Practical Urology: Essential Principles and Practice*. London: Springer, 2011. Print.

Chireau, Yvonne Patricia, and Nathaniel Deutsch. *Black Zion: African American Religious Encounters with Judaism*. New York: Oxford UP, 2000. Print.

Clutch. "Mellody Hobson Discusses How She's Unapologetically Black." *Clutch Magazine RSS*. Sutton New Media LLC, 2014. Web. 12 Mar. 2016.

Coates, Ta-Nehisi. *Between the World and Me*. New York: Spiegel & Grau, 2015. Print.

"College Campuses Call For 'Safe Spaces.'" *NPR*. NPR, 16 Nov. 2015. Web. 12 Mar. 2016.

Collins, Lisa Gail, and Margo Natalie Crawford. *New Thoughts on the Black Arts Movement*. New Brunswick, NJ: Rutgers UP, 2006. Print.

Dash, Stacey. "How Racially Skewed Are the Oscars Really?" *Stacey Dash*. Patheos, 5 Feb. 2016. Web. 05 Apr. 2016.

Denzin, Norman K., and Yvonna S. Lincoln. *Handbook of Qualitative Research*. Thousand Oaks, CA: Sage Publications, 2000. Print.

---. *Collecting and Interpreting Qualitative Materials*. Thousand Oaks, CA: Sage Publications, 2003. Print.

Drenth, Jelto. *The Origin of the World: Science and Fiction of the Vagina*. London: Reaktion, 2005. Print.

Evans-Pritchard, E. E. *Kinship and Marriage among the Nuer*. Oxford: Clarendon, 1990. Print.

Farrakhan, Louis. The Divine Destruction of America: Can She Avert It? *The Final Call*, 2 June 2015. Web. 11 Mar. 2016.

"Far More Whites Killed by US Police -." *The New Observer*. The New Observer, 17 Nov. 2015. Web. 11 Mar. 2016.

Farrell, Keith. "Truth About Cops Killing Blacks That Al Sharpton Doesn't Want You to Know." *The Federalist Papers*. 2015. Web. 11 Mar. 2016.

Foucault, Michel. *Madness and Civilization: A History of Insanity in the Age of Reason*. New York: Vintage, 1988. Print.

---. *The Order of Things: An Archaeology of the Human Sciences*. New York: Vintage, 1994. Print.

---. *Discipline and Punish: The Birth of the Prison*. New York: Vintage, 1995. Print.

Frayser, Suzanne G., and Thomas J. Whitby. *Studies in Human Sexuality: A Selected Guide*. Englewood, CO: Libraries Unlimited, 1995. Print.

Goldberg, Michelle. "What Is a Woman? - The New Yorker." *The New Yorker*. Conde Nast, 24 Apr. 2014. Web. 12 Mar. 2016.

Gomez, Michael Angelo. *Black Crescent: The Experience and Legacy of African Muslims in the Americas*. Cambridge: Cambridge UP, 2005. Print.

Graff, Amy. "San Francisco Neighbor Says Don't Call Thieves 'Criminals.'" SFGate. San Francisco Chronicle, 2 Nov. 2015. Web. 15 Mar. 2016.

Freud, Sigmund, James Strachey, and Peter Gay. *Civilization and Its Discontents*. New York: W.W. Norton, 1989. Print.

Hegel, Georg Wilhelm Friedrich, Arnold V. Miller, and J. N. Findlay. *Phenomenology of Spirit*. Oxford: Clarendon, 1977. Print.

Islamicdefender. "Farrakhan Admits to Malcolm X Assassination." *YouTube*. YouTube, 24 Sept. 2010. Web. 11 Mar. 2016.

"It's OK to Keep Watching Beyoncé's 'Formation' Music Video Over and Over Again." *RSS*. POPSUGAR., 9 Mar. 2016. Web. 11 Mar. 2016.

Jones, Layla A. "#Iftheygunnedmedown: How the Media Killed Michael Brown." *Philly.com*. 21 Aug. 0214. Web. 12 Mar. 2016.

"Killed By Police - 2015." *Killed By Police - 2015*. Killed By Police, 31 Dec. 2015. Web. 11 Mar. 2016.

Kipnis, Laura. "Sexual Paranoia Strikes Academe." *The Chronicle of Higher Education*. The Chronicle of Higher Education, 27 Feb. 2015. Web. 12 Mar. 2016.

Linke, Uli. *German Bodies: Race and Representation after Hitler*. New York: Routledge, 1999. Print.

Lukianoff, Greg, and Jonathan Haidt. "The Coddling of the American Mind: In the Name of Emotional Well-being, College Students Are Increasingly Demanding Protection from Words and Ideas They Don't Like. Here's Why That's Disastrous for Education—and Mental Health." *The Atlantic*. Atlantic Media Company, Sept. 2015. Web. 12 Mar. 2016.

"MALCOLM X: OUR HISTORY WAS DESTROYED BY SLAVERY." *YouTube*. YouTube, 5 Sept. 2006. Web. 11 Mar. 2016.

Malinowski, Bronislaw. Argonauts of the Western Pacific: An Account of Native Enterprise and Adventure in the Archipelagoes of Melanesian New Guinea. Prospect Heights, IL: Waveland, 1984. Print.

Martin, R. D., and Anne-Elise Martin. *Primate Origins and Evolution*: A Phylogenetic Reconstruction. Princeton, NJ: Princeton UP, 1990. Print.

Maslow, Abraham H., and Robert Frager. *Motivation and Personality*. New York: Harper and Row, 1987. Print.

"Michael Brown's Mother: 'My Son Doesn't Have a History of Violence'" *CBS St Louis*. KMOX, 26 Nov. 2014. Web. 11 Mar. 2016.

Muhammad, Alan. "Myth or High Science? Is There Evidence of Mr. Yakub?" *The Final Call*. The Final Call, 24 Oct. 2010. Web. 13 Mar. 2016.

Muhammad, Elijah. *Message to the Blackman in America*. Atlanta, GA: Messenger Elijah Muhammad Propagation Society, 1997. Print.

---. *Yakub (Jacob): The Father of Mankind*. Phoenix, AZ: Secretarius MEMPS Publications, 2002. Print.

NewsOne Now. "Dr. Cornel West: In America, To Be Successful You Can't Call Yourself Unapologetically Black [VIDEO]." *NewsOne*. Interactive One LLC, 2015. Web. 12 Mar. 2016.

O'Dwyer, Laura M., and James A. Bernauer. *Quantitative Research for the Qualitative Researcher*. Thousand Oaks, CA: Sage Publications, 2013. Print.

Ovid, and D. A. Raeburn. *Metamorphoses: A New Verse Translation*. London: Penguin, 2004. Print.

"Rad Fem ≠ TERF." *The TERFs*. 2016. Web. 12 Mar. 2016.

Reynolds, Jason, and Brendan Kiely. *All American Boys*. New York: Atheneum / Caitlyn Dlouhy, 2015. Print.

Riddle, Joshua. "New Photos of Michael Brown Paint a Different Picture than What We've Seen - Young Conservatives." *Young Conservatives*. 14 Aug. 2014. Web. 12 Mar. 2016.

Rush, James. "If They Gunned ME down What Picture Would They Use? African Americans Use Twitter to Protest the Photo of Michael Brown That Media Use of the Dead Teen." *Mail Online*. Associated Newspapers, 12 Aug. 2014. Web. 12 Mar. 2016.

Schapiro, Morton. "I'm Northwestern's President. Here's Why Safe Spaces for Students Are Important." *Washington Post*. The Washington Post, 16 Jan. 2016. Web. 12 Mar. 2016.

Schlosser, Edward. "I'm a Liberal Professor, and My Liberal Students Terrify Me." *Vox*. Vox, 03 June 2015. Web. 12 Mar. 2016.

Shulevitz, Judith. "In College and Hiding From Scary Ideas." *The New York Times*. The New York Times, 21 Mar. 2015. Web. 12 Mar. 2016.

Seuss. *The Sneetches: And Other Stories*. New York: Random House, 1961. Print.

Shi, Young, James Yin, and Ron Dorfman. *The Rape of Nanking*. Haikou Shi: Hainan Chu Ban She, 1999. Print.

Smith, Bryan. "Questions Remain After Larycia Hawkins, Wheaton College Sever Ties." *Politics & City Life*. Chicago Magazine, 11 Feb. 2016. Web. 29 Apr. 2016.
Spross, Jeff. "Mike Brown's Family Asked To See Robbery Footage Before Police Released It To Media, But Were Ignored." *ThinkProgress RSS*. 17 Aug. 2014. Web. 12 Mar. 2016.

Suk, Jeannie. "Shutting Down Conversations About Rape at Harvard Law - The New Yorker." *The New Yorker*. The New Yorker, 11 Dec. 2015. Web. 12 Mar. 2016.

"The Right to Fright." *The Economist*. The Economist Newspaper, 14 Nov. 2015. Web. 12 Mar. 2016.

Thompson, Hunter S. *Hell's Angels: A Strange and Terrible Saga*. New York: Ballantine, 1996. Print.

Vonnegut, Kurt. *Mother Night*. New York: Delta Trade Paperbacks, 1999. Print.

"Watch: Beyoncé Crushing the Super Bowl 50 Halftime Show." *Vox*. Vox Culture, 07 Feb. 2016. Web. 11 Mar. 2016.

White, Penny. "Why I No Longer Hate 'TERFs' - Feminist Current." *Feminist Current*. Feminist Current, 10 Nov. 2015. Web. 12 Mar. 2016.

Wray, T. J., and Gregory Mobley. *The Birth of Satan: Tracing the Devil's Biblical Roots*. New York: Palgrave Macmillan, 2005. Print.

X, Malcolm, and Alex Haley. *The Autobiography of Malcolm X*. New York: Ballantine, 2015. Print.

CPSIA information can be obtained
at www.ICGtesting.com
Printed in the USA
BVHW041307050321
601826BV00018B/213